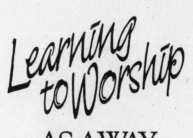

Learning to Worship

AS A WAY
OF LIFE

LINCOLN CHRISTIAN COLLEGE AND SEMINARY

P9-DIG-884

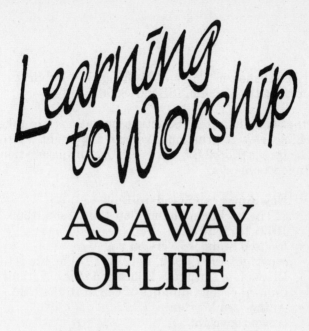

Learning to Worship

AS A WAY OF LIFE

Graham Kendrick

BETHANY HOUSE PUBLISHERS

MINNEAPOLIS, MINNESOTA 55438

A Division of Bethany Fellowship, Inc.

Originally published in England by Kingsway Publications Limited under the title *Worship*, ISBN 0–86065–274–2.

Unless otherwise indicated, Scripture quotations are taken from the Holy Bible, New International Version. Copyright © 1973, 1978, 1984 by the International Bible Society. Used by permission of Zondervan Bible Publishers.

NASB = New American Standard Bible
      © The Lockman Foundation 1960, 1962, 1963, 1968
      1971, 1972, 1973
RSV = Revised Standard Version
      copyright 1946, 1952, © 1971, 1973 by the
      Division of Christian Education of the National
      Council of the Churches of Christ in the USA
AV = Authorized Version
      crown copyright

Copyright © 1984
Graham Kendrick
All Rights Reserved

Published by Bethany House Publishers
A Division of Bethany Fellowship, Inc.
6820 Auto Club Road, Minneapolis, MN 55438

Printed in the United States of America

Library of Congress Cataloging in Publication Data

Kendrick, Graham.
    Learning to worship as a way of life.

    Original title: Worship.
    1. Public worship.   I. Title.
BV15.K45   1985   264   85–9151
ISBN 0–87123–863–2

TO
the women in my life—
my wife Jill and daughters Abigail,
Amy and Tamsin

52'

88549

GRAHAM KENDRICK is a Christian leader and songwriter, known across England for his many songs of praise and worship. He has had many years of experience in leading worship, both in small and large gatherings. He and his wife make their home south of London.

Contents

'It is not good to have zeal without knowledge.'

Prov 19:2

1

Celebrating the Truth about God

Who are we all hiding from?

It was the little boy's first trip to church, and his mother had hurriedly put him through the correct 'Sunday best' procedure of thorough washing, dressing in smart clothes, and the inventing of a parting in his hair—previously unknown to his startled scalp. Having been warned to 'behave', which generally meant 'shut up and don't fidget', they proceeded to the local church under the incessant clanging of its bell.

On entering the church, the boy was instantly curious, fascinated by this strange new world. The hushed voices, the high arches, the slightly musty smell and the rows of empty wooden pews. Or were they empty? No, here and there a hat, the back of a head, a pair of hunched shoulders, would bob up or down, appear or disappear.

His mother led him in whispers to one of these dark tunnel-like rows, where she immediately knelt and bowed her head; he copied instinctively. The silence only lasted for a few more seconds, as the question that had been growing more and more urgent in his lively young mind suddenly burst out, ringing loud and clear through the ancient arches: 'Mummy, who are we all hiding from?'

The ensuing scene, the embarrassment and the retribu-
tions that may have befallen the boy are better left to the
imagination, but it is worth pondering upon the irony of
his analysis of the situation.

Who *were* they hiding from, or rather, why did their
behaviour give the lad that impression? No doubt later on
in the service (unless he was removed of course) the boy
would have heard some singing, some readings from
Scripture, a sermon, responses and so on, but I wonder if
that first impression would have been totally dispelled by
the end of the proceedings. What I am sure of is that he
did not leave that building with a sense of wonder, excitement and awe, trembling at his first experience of being
caught in the very presence of God, as the worshippers
enthroned the living God in their gathering, upon wave
after wave of spontaneous heartfelt praise and worship. I
am sure that he did not look up at joy-filled faces or see
sad ones released from their worry and fear and transformed before his eyes into expressions of happiness,
peace and serenity. What I am also pretty sure of is that by
the end the little boy was rather bored and wondering
what he was missing on telly. In fact he was probably
reduced to feeling much the same as a good many other
churchgoers that morning.

I can well remember in my own childhood how going to
church seemed so often to be little more than a lesson in
patience and endurance. I longed for 'the service' to come
to an end. I would watch the dust floating in the shafts of
summer sunlight, or scratch with my 'collection penny' in
the varnish of the pew in front of me. The trouble was,
nothing ever *happened*; well, certain prescribed things did,
but nothing unexpected or unusual—unless somebody
fainted, or had a fit, or knocked over a pile of hymnbooks.

A God who never does anything?

Years and years of churchgoing taught me much about God and the Bible, and I would be wrong to underestimate the important truths and concepts that penetrated my mind. Yet, in a subtle but powerful way, I unconsciously began to believe, in total contradiction to my stated beliefs, that God is a God who never does anything. Oh, certainly he *used* to do things, and undoubtedly still did do things abroad through missionaries and in the lives of people who then wrote books about it. But to do anything tangible, real or supernatural, here and now?—that would have really scared us! Actually, I think most of us would have been delighted, having got over the initial shock.

It is interesting to note that many years later, when spiritual hunger demanded to be satisfied, my biggest barrier to entering into any experience of the Spirit of God was this pervading unbelief arising out of twenty years or so of apparent divine inactivity. I found myself trapped by a subconscious conviction that 'nothing will ever happen to me'. Of course it was in no way God's fault, and unbeknown to me at that time God was stirring his people into a dynamic awareness of his life-changing power and glory. But that is another part of the story.

A taste of heaven

Returning to our little boy for a moment, let us consider what the reality should have been. In 1 Peter 2:9 we read, 'But you are a chosen people, a royal priesthood, a holy nation, a people belonging to God, that you may declare the praises of him who called you out of darkness into his wonderful light.' The New American Standard Bible uses the phrase 'that you may proclaim the excellencies of him who has called you'. Here we see something of the marvellous plan of God for his church. He has chosen us for a reason, elevated us to a status beyond our imagination, called us together as a new eternal nation for a very definite purpose. We are to proclaim his excellencies, declare his praise.

Sometimes it seems that once we are forgiven for our sins, the 'great transaction' done and our salvation secure in terms of an entrance ticket to heaven, we slip our ticket into our back pocket and sit on it until we reach our final destination. Thus we endure our spiritual bus journey, passing the time looking out of the window and chatting to our fellow passengers.

Thankfully, this passive view of salvation is less and less in evidence today, and recent years have seen an ever-broadening understanding of God's plan to redeem our whole personalities, our relationships and finally the whole of creation. The climax of the Scriptures indeed shows us just that, and in the book of Revelation we see glimpses of a totally new order, not only 'spiritual' but physical and tangible. And worship is the dominant and all-consuming activity of the redeemed millions and countless angelic beings. Revelation 19:5–7 says:

> Then a voice came from the throne saying: 'Praise our God, all you his servants, you who fear him, both small and great!' Then I heard what sounded like a great multitude, like the roar of rushing waters and like loud peals of thunder, shouting: 'Hallelujah! For the Lord God Almighty reigns. Let us rejoice and be glad and give him glory!'

A glorious destiny

Worship is our destination, and there is no doubt that praise and worship should be the dominant feature of the journey there. Our praise and worship begins now, not then. They just get perfected somewhat when we arrive! Ephesians 1:11–12 says:

In him we were also chosen, having been predestined according to the plan of him who works out everything in conformity with the purpose of his will, in order that we, who were the first to hope in Christ, might be for the praise of his glory.

We are chosen, predestined, planned and willed by God himself to this very end!

The Westminster Shorter Catechism, in what can be seen as a kind of summing up of these and other scriptures, states, 'Man's chief end is to glorify God and enjoy him for ever.' The nature of our future heavenly worship is marvellous to ponder on, though it must be realized that we can only begin to know anything about it through the use of comparisons with things that are familiar to us. Yet we do have a foretaste, a kind of down payment on this future glory. Ephesians 1:13–14 goes on to say:

Having believed, you were marked in him with a seal, the promised Holy Spirit, who is a deposit guaranteeing our inheritance until the redemption of those who are God's possession—to the praise of his glory.

It is the joy of many millions of Christians across the world to experience the 'streams of living water' from the Holy Spirit within, overflowing into magnificent worship to the Father, and this is just a hint of what is to come!

A friend of mine when asked why he dances in worship of God says, 'I dance because I can't fly!' If we feel down here that for safety reasons we sometimes ought to nail our boots to the floor, then what might be in store for us in the future! There may be jobs going for heavenly air traffic controllers as people like my friend finally realize their ambition! I like to think of the saints meeting their Lord at the second coming that way too, a worldwide company of worshippers that can't be held down any longer!

Our present concern, however, is to get ready for heaven, and to introduce heavenly practices on earth so that we can truly pray, 'Your kingdom come, your will be done on earth as it is in heaven.' Our preoccupation should not be with denominational preferences, matters of style, tradition, personal taste or fashion, but with the revealed will of God, 'that you may proclaim the excellencies of him who has called you out of darkness into his marvellous light'.

Praise should match its object

So what does it mean in practice to proclaim his excellencies or declare his praises? Is this command totally satisfied by what normally goes on between certain set hours every Sunday? If there is one thing that the British are good at, despite our traditional reserve and emotional conservation, it is pomp and ceremony. We really are very expert at it, as evidenced by events such as the wedding of the Prince and Princess of Wales. The greater in standing the people involved, the more significant the occasion, the more splendid and ornate the celebration. The organizers demand that the event should match the importance of the personalities featured and the majesty they are meant to represent. On a more mundane level, we all carry out this same principle in our family and social lives. Heroes from the Falklands conflict were welcomed back to their council houses or surburban streets with banners, singing, shouting and cheering. Weddings are celebrated as special events and the couple praised by proud parents; new babies are doted upon and their parents congratulated. Young people passing exams are given presents and applauded at ceremonies for their achievements, and at football matches even British people go wild with excitement as they praise their winning team, lifting the hero of the match on their shoulders in a victory parade, shouting or dancing themselves to exhaustion! We somehow feel that it is only right that the praise should match the importance of the person, their achievement or the occasion, even if the occasion only amounts to twenty-two men kicking a sphere of inflated leather round a muddy field!

Precisely the same principle is appropriate to our Creator God, and yet infinitely more so. Our earthly objects of praise are often unworthy of it, and frequently praised for quite the wrong reasons. God, however, is totally worthy of the praise and worship of his whole creation. He would be totally worthy of it even if he had chosen to condemn the whole human race for our sin and rebellion, without any hope of salvation, let alone his immeasurable praiseworthiness for his love in providing through his Son that marvellous hope.

The principle here is that our praise and worship should attempt to match its object. I say 'attempt' because even an eternity of praise will never do justice to the attributes and character of God, but each fresh new aeon will discover something yet more exhilarating, and another explosion of vibrant heartfelt celebration will burst across the new heaven and earth and echo to the corners of the new creation. Is there not, then, something desperately wrong if we get regularly bored in church? Do we think that the only appropriate way to worship God is to never stray from the tram-lines of liturgical rigidity (whether conformist or non-conformist!), physical rigidity, and mental rigidity, with everything predictable and undemanding? Does this match in any way our Saviour and God? What kind of a God do we think we have? Is he not endlessly creative, irrepressibly vital and alive, always doing 'new things'. Indeed God is 'the same yesterday, today and for ever', but one of his unchanging characteristics is that he is always full of surprises! If the presence of God is made known in our worship, if his Living Presence truly saturates the proceedings, then not only will there be the reverence and order that characterize the holy God of an ordered creation, but a sense of the unexpected that reflects his endless creativity as he moulds and fashions our lives together.

God in a box

People who have been to see *The Sound of Music* at the cinema umpteen times, almost religiously you might say, obviously derive some pleasure from it on each successive occasion. Quite what it is that keeps them going defies my power of understanding, but I accept that such people exist! I would imagine that even these *aficionados* will eventually (if they have not already atrophied in their seats) get tired of the same old lines, knowing exactly how the story will end. Elements of suspense and surprise, such as they are, must eventually disappear almost entirely. The same numbing effect is frequently achieved among 'worshippers', where the god who is worshipped is a god of the past, who fits neatly into the box of our predetermined patterns and, to the great relief of many, never does anything remotely unexpected, never causes his servants to move beyond the bounds of what is humanly explainable, and never does anything supernatural.

If this is the God who is being worshipped, then it is patently not the God of the Scriptures. It must be a false one, or at the very least a false image superimposed like a photo-negative upon the real God, obscuring his true dynamic nature, hiding his breathtaking and awesome power.

Telling lies about God

Hence, I would dare to say that many of our patterns and practices of worship, in a subtle but nevertheless effective manner, tell lies about God. Could it not be seen as a terribly sad but natural result of this kind of deadness in worship that some years ago it was proclaimed by Nietzsche: 'God is dead.' The irony of that gigantically presumptuous statement is borne out by the subsequent rash of popular graffiti that proclaimed: '*God is dead*, signed Nietzsche' and underneath '*Nietzsche is dead*, signed God'. It was never God that died, but who can blame the agnostic and atheistic—and even the ecclesiastical world—for coming to this conclusion when they observe the worship of the people whose final destiny and present purpose is to 'proclaim the excellencies of him who has called you out of darkness into his marvellous light'. It was so true when A. W. Tozer said, 'The church is more guilty of not being revived than the world is of not being converted.' Judgement begins at the house of God; we are those without the excuse of ignorance. There are many other lies about God which may sadly be propagated by observing some kinds of Christian 'worship'. I even hesitate to put them in print because they are such damnable lies: God is boring; God is irrelevant; God is powerless. He is none of these things and it is time that we demonstrated in our worship the truth about God, and sent the lies back to where they came from.

2

What Is Worship?

It may seem elementary to ask the question 'What is worship?' but it is surprising how little understanding there is among Christians of this most fundamental part of our humanity. Is it something religious people do on Sundays? Is it a funny internal feeling that makes you want to sing? Is it an activity for Christians of a certain emotional disposition? Is it a word to describe everything in a church service that leads up to the sermon? A pleasant corporate activity involving community singing of favourite choruses? Should it be loud or quiet, and should it be organ and choir or drums and guitars?

Opinion, it seems, will never cease to vary, along with fads, fashions and factions, as to how worship should be conducted, but it seems remarkable to me that so much of the conversation, discussion and disagreement about worship is actually concerned with our own personal preferences. One person prefers traditional hymns, another sings only new choruses. Someone else will not attend a service unless it is the 1662 prayerbook version, yet another will not come unless she is free to raise her hands and dance, while her husband won't come with her because she might! A neutral observer to these disputes might easily go away believing that worship is conducted purely for the benefit and satisfaction of the participants. Regrettably, there is often some truth in this for the question as to what we are trying to achieve through these means is rarely asked.

Worship is for God. He is our Creator, and the worship of his creatures is both his right and his pleasure. Worship is first and foremost for his benefit, not ours, though it is marvellous to discover that in giving him pleasure, we ourselves enter into what can become our richest and most wholesome experience in life. It would be quite reasonable of God to demand our worship, as a right and a duty, without any pleasure to ourselves, but it is a glorious truth about him that he wants worship to be a relationship of giving from both directions. It is surely a tragedy when the pleasure we receive, and the satisfaction of our own tastes and preferences, become the whole object of the exercise. The manner in which we worship is of course of great importance to us, but our foremost consideration must be what gives pleasure and glory to the One who is the object of our worship.

Worship is God's enjoyment of us and our enjoyment of him. In Psalm 149:2–4 we read, 'Let Israel be glad in his maker; let the people of Zion rejoice in their King. Let them praise His name with dancing; let them sing praises to Him with timbrel and lyre. For the Lord takes pleasure in His people' (NASB). It comes as a startling revelation to many of us that we are able to give God pleasure. Surely it is a most wonderful mystery that an individual human being, whoever or whatever he may be, has the potential for giving joy to the Creator of the universe! How many of us draw back from this truth into a sense of our own insignificance, disbelieving that anyone so cosmically important as God can be the least bit interested in our meagre offerings? Yet it is gloriously true, and fundamental to the whole gospel of Jesus Christ, that God's intention was not just to save us from hell and judgement (though all believers will be eternally grateful for that!) but to bear, by way of the new birth of the Spirit, children into his family: sons and daughters enjoying an intimate personal relationship with their heavenly Father.

Worth-ship

The origin in English of the word 'worship' is 'worth-ship', which expresses the value placed on someone or something. The true quality and depth of our love for God will to a very great degree be evidenced by the quality and depth of our worship. When we value somebody, we do things to demonstrate that love; we put our thanks, appreciation and adoration into words, we give gifts and show that we care in practical ways. Indeed how often do we hear the complaint, 'You say you love me, but you never show it.' Talk is cheap, but actions do speak louder than words and are a test of whether our words are genuine.

It was an important discovery for me some years ago, when I found out the full meaning of the original Greek word which is used most often in the New Testament and translated as 'worship'. In fact, there are seven Greek words: five of these occur once, another occurs three times, but the final one appears no less than fifty-nine times. This word is *proskyneo*, and its overwhelming use compared to the other words must tell us something of its importance. The basic meaning is 'to come towards to kiss (the hand)' and it denotes both the external act of prostrating oneself in worship and the corresponding inward attitude of reverence and humility (*New International Dictionary of the New Testament*, Paternoster Press 1978). This gives us a beautiful picture of worship as we approach the King of kings and Lord of lords; with open face, eye to eye, our hearts full of love and thanks, our wills set firmly to obey him, enjoying an intimacy and a mutual affection that the watching angels find astounding. Considering that in heaven's eyes we were once rebels and sworn enemies, originally made in God's perfect image yet twisted into grotesque parodies by sin, this is incredible!

Where does worship begin?

Everybody worships. Whether it is a hero, possessions, success, pleasure, a political cause, a carved idol or one-self, the way we live and behave makes evident the things we love and give ourselves to. It is in our very nature to worship, and that inner drive is God-given; the disaster is that as part of a fallen race, we have replaced the object of our worship. To be converted to faith in Jesus Christ is to return to the worship of the true God, and to dethrone all rivals to his authority. The very heart of worship is the giving, not only of our talents and goods, but of our very selves.

In Romans 12:1 the apostle Paul teaches, 'Therefore, I urge you, brothers, in view of God's mercy, to offer your bodies as living sacrifices, holy and pleasing to God—which is your spiritual worship.' Spiritual worship should not be misunderstood as something ephemeral and abstract; instead, it starts with ownership of the body. Who do I belong to? To whom should I devote my energies, muscular, mental, and spiritual?

A living sacrifice

It would be easy to pass over the term 'living sacrifice' too quickly and miss the paradox created by putting those two words side by side. To Paul's thoroughly Jewish mind, steeped in the tradition of his fathers and saturated by the Old Testament scriptures, a sacrifice was clearly one thing—it was dead. It was most likely a sheep whose throat had been cut, its life ended, offered up to God to atone for sin. Now Paul knew that in Christ full atonement had been made once and for all, but the sense of the finality of being totally offered up to God is strongly present in this picture. The animal was not a sacrifice until it was dead, so to talk of a 'living sacrifice' is on the face of it a contradiction. This is not the only place in Romans where Paul puts side by side concepts of being alive and dead at the same time. In chapter 6 verses 11–13 he says:

> Count yourselves dead to sin but alive to God in Christ Jesus.... Do not offer the parts of your body to sin, as instruments of wickedness, but rather offer yourselves to God as those who have been brought from death to life; and offer the parts of your body to him as instruments of righteousness.

Alive to God—together

This passage in Romans is at the very heart of worship, and it is the heart that God searches to see whether we are dying daily to our own selfish ways, and are therefore alive with the life and power of Jesus. If this is true of us, then every thought, action and emotion can become an act of true worship. It is evident that where a body of Christians are living like this, gatherings for worship take on a new freshness and vitality, and the problem of leadership becomes more a matter of channelling the flow, and stopping things from getting out of hand! There are things to praise *about*, answered prayers to give thanks for and be happy about, stories to relate of God's activity since the last meeting, and lessons about learning to share together. A gathering for worship is no more an act of worship than being a loving mother and housewife, or practising hospitality, or doing your job well (provided these are being done to the glory of God); it is simply a special time when we lay aside the necessary but mundane activities of life and give our whole energy and attention to *expressing* what has become fundamental to our lives. Weary minds can be refreshed and set free in thoughts about God. Our bodies, tense and tired after being hunched over a desk, a machine, the kitchen sink, or the steering wheel of a car can relax, loosen up and get ready to express our response to the presence of a loving God in every part of our lives.

A token of the whole

Meetings for corporate worship can of necessity only be engaged in occasionally; the business of life and work guarantees that. Those times, special though they are, are really just a token of the fact that all of life belongs to, and is being offered up daily in thanksgiving to, the Creator. It is like the wedding ring given as a token of the giving of one person to another in marriage, or the giving of a gift to demonstrate love and esteem.

Repentance is worship

The genuineness of our worship, however, cannot be measured in decibels of sound, and although it is vital that we express our love for God vocally, he looks to see the evidence in our lives. We do not always think of repentance as worship, but it can be much easier to sing a rousing hymn than to turn away from our favourite sin. A sinful act involves worship of the wrong kind, submitting ourselves at that moment to serve the appetites of our pride or lust, and so repentance is literally a transfer of our worship back to the One who rightfully owns it. It is significant that during Jesus' temptation in the wilderness, Satan used the word *proskyneo* (denoting a kiss of worship, as we have seen) when tempting Jesus by offering him all the kingdoms of the world and their glory if only he would bow down and worship him. Worship has been misunderstood as something that arises from a feeling which 'comes upon you', but it is vital that we understand that it is rooted in a conscious act of the will, to serve and obey the Lord Jesus Christ. The feelings, the joy of having been forgiven, follow on as a consequence of our reunion with him.

Work is worship

In Colossians 3:23–24 we are told, 'Whatever you do, work at it with all your heart, as working for the Lord, not for men.... It is the Lord Christ you are serving.' How hard it seems to vacuum the carpet for the ten thousandth time, or wash up, or lift another packing-case, or whatever it is we wish we did not have to do, for the Lord! And yet, if we relegate worship to services and meetings, we are in danger of living in a kind of spiritual schizophrenia, shutting off the greater part of our lives from being offered to the Lord who fills all of life.

Don't give up!

Worship, then, is at heart a person offered to God, claiming no rights, making no more selfish demands than a dead man does, but living fully, richly and wholly to God and by his power. To be honest, even as I write it, I know that this sometimes seems beyond reach, and yet God is able to get us there despite our kicking and struggling and running away, and I comfort myself that he has many times succeeded with far more hopeless cases than me! Even when we have begun, it doesn't happen overnight; it happens over *life*, and meanwhile our heavenly Father's patience and tenderness are inexhaustible. He takes us as we are, where we are; to be realistic, where else can we start?

Not my will—but yours

As in all things, our best example of a life of worship is Jesus, whose every breath was breathed, every meal eaten and every word spoken in natural relaxed worship of God. As a child, my concept of Jesus was a strange mixture of ideas. The Sunday School pictures didn't help much either. Most of them portrayed a golden-haired, blue-eyed man, not Jewish at all, who seemed to glow all over, particularly around the face and head, and while I understand the artist's attempt to signify the divinity of Christ in this way, the effect was to create an image of a respectable, westernized Christ who was somehow unreal, even ghostly. The image in so many minds is one of a white-robed, almost floating figure blessing people to the accompaniment of distant angelic choirs. Hollywood has a lot to answer for!

But the point is that Jesus was really human. He was really God too, but we are told that he laid aside his heavenly glory and became in all respects as a man (though never less than God), experiencing our human condition, except for committing sin, even as far as a cruel and ignominious death. What we so easily forget is his experience of humanity: his thirty years in that run-down infamous town of Nazareth; his sweated labour in the workshop; the cuts and scars of his calloused hands; the meals he ate, the washing-up, the shopping, the daily grind and no luxuries! And later on, during those three years with his disciples, the weariness such that he was not even wakened by a storm, the times of fun and laughter with his friends, their meals together and the stories they told one another. The dirt and dust, the happiness and the tears and, in the end, desertion and betrayal.

The question has often been asked, and I will ask it again: was Jesus' life more offered up to God when he was healing the sick, or when he was eating his breakfast? Was it more acceptable to his Father when he was preaching in the synagogues, or when he was enjoying a rough and tumble with his friends? Was he more holy when he was transfigured on the mountain and spoke with Moses and Elijah, or when he spat on the ground to make clay to rub on a blind man's eyes?

Worship in the mundane

The answer is that his whole life was an act of worship, including the most mundane and basic elements of being a human being, and all of it was pleasing to his Father. In fact, it was even before he had begun his three years of preaching and miracles that his Father proclaimed over him at his baptism: 'This is my beloved son in whom I am well pleased.' Surely at that time the Father must have been referring not only to his obedience in baptism, but also to the previous thirty years spent in obscurity and 'the mundane'!

The worship of the will

If, however, we were to attempt to choose an incident in Jesus' earthly life that seems most vividly to illustrate his worship of God, where might our final choice lead us? When might his heart of hearts be most exposed and revealed? The truth about us is surely never more clearly exhibited than when we are under intense pressure. It is then that our true character cannot hide because everything that overlays or embellishes it is stripped away.

I don't think that there can be much doubt as to the time of Jesus' greatest pressure. The scene in the Garden of Gethsemane shows him in such agony of spirit that he said: 'My soul is overwhelmed with sorrow to the point of death.' We read that: 'being in anguish, he prayed more earnestly, and his sweat was like drops of blood falling to the ground'. Yet despite the terrible ordeal that he knew was ahead of him, and the sorrow that itself nearly killed him, he prayed to his Father: 'yet not what I will, but what you will'.

I have heard this scene described as the greatest example of worship in the whole Bible. Obedience is worship, and without obedience to God we cannot truly worship him. However enthusiastic or 'liberated' our participation in worship may be, unless in the reality of daily living, we have offered ourselves to God, and truly belong to him, it will be no more than wasted energy and meaningless noise. Let us beware of the danger of attempting to renew our forms of worship when our daily lives are evidence that our bodies are not offered up on the altar as a 'living sacrifice'.

3

Dethroning the Gods

Worship is not just a matter of what happens between set hours on a Sunday. If we fail to realize this, we are fooling ourselves. It is not even a question of whether it is ancient or modern, staid or enthusiastic, creative or boring. What we so often fail to recognize is that worship is at the very heart of a radically different way of living. To adopt new freedoms of expression—new music, dance, drama and so on in our worship—is by no means to guarantee the reality of it or its acceptability to God, and in many places we are in serious danger of mistaking these outward developments for true worship in the sight of God. To worship implies far more than participation in a series of devotional acts at regular intervals.

Even when we talk comfortably in terms of presenting our very selves as living sacrifices, feeling that we have understood this as being true worship, I wonder whether even then we have seen its full implications. This is because of a popular tendency to 'spiritualize' our faith at the cost of 'earthing it', of abstracting it rather than seeing it right through to its practical application. Of course the worship that the Father desires is worship 'in spirit', but we must remind ourselves that the Bible sees us as whole people, and consequently a 'spiritual' act can never be separated from simultaneous actions in the body. Thus 'spiritual' activities that bear no relationship to the way in which we live our everyday lives are shown to be at best little more than sentiment, and at worst, blatant hypocrisy. (This argument is developed more fully in Chapter 9.)

Spiritual self-gratification

It is also far too easy, within the current upsurge of creative input in the realm of worship, to find ourselves chasing spiritual or aesthetic experiences, as if the highest achievement of our whole pilgrimage on earth was to enter some kind of praise-induced ecstasy! I am in fact all in favour of spiritual experiences when they are genuine, and welcome ecstasies that are gifts of God and not artificially induced, but if such things become the *aim* of our gatherings for worship, then we have turned the gospel upside down. The gospel is for the salvation of the world, and we are sometimes in danger of locking ourselves inside the rescue-shop and plundering the stock of blessings for the sole purpose of spiritual self-gratification, while millions stream empty-handed past the closed doors into eternal darkness, hearing the joyful sounds and seeing the advertisements, but never being given a chance to test the goods.

Worshipping in a fallen world

There is a desperate need to place renewed forms of worship in the wider context of what worship is, and to work through the social, economic and political implications that worshipping God inevitably creates. Worship, or rather misdirected worship, is in fact the issue at the very heart of the world's problems. It should be obvious that worship is not the exclusive property of the Christian, or of the adherents to other religious faiths. The practice of worship is an inescapable part of being human; even an atheist is a worshipper of something, because there is built into all of us the vacuum left by our loss of communion with God that took place at the Fall. We were created to worship, and having rejected the rightful worthy object of all worship, mankind has continued through his sad history, substituting every variety of false god, and serving successions of them in fear and misery.

The gods we worship

The gods of present-day Western society may not be so obvious as the gods of wood, stone and metal that sit in shrines and on mantelpieces (although it is amazing how well even they survive in a supposedly enlightened age). The subtlety of our modern gods probably makes them even more dangerous.

There is the god of affluence, to whom we sacrifice our energy, time and health in an effort to make him smile upon us and keep us in the manner to which we are determined to remain (or become!) accustomed.

There is the god of personal happiness and fulfilment, to whom we will sacrifice apparently unsuitable marriage partners and as many unpleasant and restricting duties and responsibilities as possible, and in whose honour we will chase endless fads, fantasies and quasi-religious practices (from horoscopes to transcendental meditation) in order to find the door to his elusive temple.

There is the dark foreboding god of fear, whom we attempt to appease with offerings of tranquillizers, unnaturally protective relationships and maybe even insurance policies.

There are the gods of unjust social systems to whom we

continue to permit the sacrifice of the helpless and the poor, and whose shrines we are willing to protect by the use of military force if necessary.

We could add to this abbreviated list the large-scale gods of nationalism, racism and culture and the personal gods of pride, lust, ambition and the like. It would be naive to think that we can easily disentangle ourselves from these objects of worship, because as part of a world system that has exchanged the one true god for many 'gods', we have all been brought up, at least to some degree, to bow down and worship them. The ones that involve the most obvious sins may quickly be identified and dethroned when we become Christians, but the ones that more easily escape our attention do so because they have become so intricately woven into the whole fabric of the social, cultural and national context in which we live, that we simply cannot see them.

The renewing of the mind

It is only as we worship God intelligently and spiritually, constantly adjusting our focus to a clearer definition of his character and deeds, that the false gods are exposed for what they are, and we are more able to extricate ourselves—or rather, we find ourselves being extricated—from their destructive influence. The passage in Romans 12:1 about presenting our bodies as living sacrifices, goes on to say: 'Do not conform any longer to the pattern of this world, but be transformed by the renewing of your mind.' Each time that we set aside for praising and enjoying God we are able to shake off a little more of the conformity to the world that clings to us, not by desperately trying to shake it off (which can become a negative activity) but by absorbing our whole selves—body, mind, spirit and emotions—in God himself and adjusting our view of the world to conform to his.

Knowing how God feels

By filling our vision with him, we leave less and less room for other gods, and we are less and less deceived by them. Entering into the 'courts of God' we may also understand more of his feelings about the systems we are part of, how he views our domestic and national economies in relation to the poor, how he reacts to injustice, violence and so on. If worship can be rightly thought of as looking with unveiled face into the Lord's face, then we should expect to see his expressions as he looks at his world, and indeed as he looks into our own faces. If true worship involves knowing God as our Father, then we must expect a fatherly discipline to accompany our worship, as he lovingly but firmly corrects our attitudes and behaviour. He will also teach us to conform to his fatherly love, and put within us some of the painful feelings of a Father who watches many of his children suffer in captivity, or pain or poverty, with few prepared to help them.

Worship is a political act

How often do we blandly sing 'Jesus is Lord!' in apparent blindness to the implications of that enormous statement? To genuinely worship Jesus as Lord of all is immediately to challenge all false gods, and to pose a threat to their dark and dingy domains. Bearing in mind that the gods of this world are intricately bound into the godless political and social systems that surround us, it is absolutely true to say that worship is a political act. If Jesus is Lord, then every other 'lord' is excluded from that title and subservient to him.

For many of the early Christians, to voice the glorious

affirmation 'Jesus is Lord' was to pronounce their own sentence of death. Such a statement, linked to a life that practised Christ's lordship, was seen as an act of political treason and punished as such.

We have similar situations today under strict atheistic regimes where a denial of the 'lordship' of the state is treated as a treasonable offence because it undermines the very ideological foundations upon which the security of such states are built. It is true that, in Western 'free' society, the cry 'Jesus is Lord!' is all too often ignored by the authorities, but that should not in any way be taken as a sign that democratic states acknowledge or tolerate his lordship! Closer to the truth would be the explanation that our presence in society reflects so little of the radical challenge of the statement that we are tolerated as a peculiar but fairly harmless sect.

A rival kingdom

To give one small but down-to-earth example, the erosion of standards of honesty in Britain has taken on the proportions of a landslide, and a 'black economy' exists at every level of society involving such practices as tax evasion, petty theft, bribes and back-handers, minor and major fraud, and every kind of 'fiddling' from exaggerated statements of business expenses to the falsifying of time-sheets. By 'turning a blind eye' and compromising, a Christian employee can coexist happily with his workmates (if not with his conscience!), but the moment he acknowledges the God of truth as Lord, and refuses to join the system, the knives come out. In such a system, an honest man is an embarrassment and must be 'normalized' or disposed of! On a wider scale, a community of God's people need only to take a stand on an issue such as abortion, having come under the lordship of a God who says 'you shall not kill' and seen his anger and grief over the mass murder of the unborn, and a stream of vitriolic condemnation flies forth from the pro-abortionists and their sympathizers. To worship Jesus as Lord is not only to invite his lordship into our individual lives but to set up a rival kingdom in the middle of the old one, which inevitably invites the wrath of the 'gods' down upon our heads.

A vision of Christ

It seems that the church has often veered from one emphasis to the other, from an almost exclusive concern for its own health and 'spirituality' to a neglect of personal experience of God and his power for the sake of social and political activism. In the first case the result has often been a separatist 'ghetto' mentality, with the church falling inwards on itself, and in the second case the genuine power and experience of God has been abandoned for something that in practice is only marginally discernible from humanism or socialism. Where both these 'camps' exist, neither seems to make much impact upon the world. What we need is not a compromise, or even a union of the best of both, but a constantly renewed vision and experience of Christ. From all our activities, battles and campaigns, we need constantly to return to worship the greatest Champion of the poor and oppressed, of truth and justice, Christ himself. In him we discover the true motive for changing society, which is not our own idealism, despair, frustration or self-image as would-be 'liberators', but the God who says 'Be holy because I, the Lord your God, am holy' (Lev 19:2). It is in worship that we concentrate our attention upon the One who laid down his life for the world, and trusted neither in the power of political activism, nor in mystical escapism under the title of 'spirituality'.

We Christians are in the business of building the kingdom of God on earth, in expectation of its culmination in an eternal kingdom; but if this kingdom does not have its roots in heaven right now, it will turn out to be little different from the world's kingdom which will not survive the 'shaking of all things'. Only that which cannot be shaken will remain, and surely anything that does not have its roots in heaven, and in the worship of heaven, will not continue into eternity.

Joy in the midst of sorrow

There are those who claim that they cannot with a clear conscience worship God in joy and celebration while there is misery and injustice in the world, and though it is easy to understand their emotions, we must remember that Jesus lived in the middle of a suffering world and was spoken of prophetically in the following way: 'Your throne, O God, will last for ever and ever; a sceptre of justice will be the sceptre of your kingdom. You love righteousness and hate wickedness; therefore God, your God, has set you above your companions by anointing you with the oil of joy' (Ps 45:6–7). There is here a direct connection between the rule of justice, the love of righteousness and hatred of wickedness, and being outstanding in the experience of joy! Joy is an authentic expression of worship and this passage shows us that the King of this new kingdom is living in a unity of spiritual and social activity.

Because we love the King

Many of us are worshipping the King in apparent ignorance or disregard of the justice and righteousness of his kingdom, while others are trying to build the kingdom while neglecting to worship the King. The King and his kingdom are inseparable, the kingdom being no less than a practical extension of his character, and we must not forget that it is built for his glory anyway! We should build the kingdom because we love and worship the King, or we may discover too late that we have been building not *his* kingdom, but ours.

The implications of worshipping God in a world of false gods are numerous and costly. Worship is a new way of living, and we inevitably feel the violence of its pull as we turn against the tide. Yet in the very act of worship—from the setting of the will to obey in a small matter of truth or honesty, to the exercise of the spirit and voice in corporate praise—there are tremendous resources of strength, healing and inspiration to be found.

It is 'Christ in us' who is the 'hope of glory', our hope and the world's hope, and it is in lifting him up that those without hope are drawn to him. There is no doubt that our forms of worship can be used to misdirect us into a false spirituality that cuts us off from the outside world, and many may have become disillusioned or critical of it for that very reason.

Worship, however—that is, an encounter with the living, caring, suffering Christ—will always send us out into the world to be more like him. Our motive for changing the world must be Jesus himself; his example, his teaching, his sacrificial giving of himself, and his presence inside us by the Holy Spirit. It is only his love in us that can possibly bear the crushing load of problems and pain that face us as we try to reach out. It is our love affair with him that gives us inspiration to love others, and his lordship in our lives that is the only power that has ever overcome the world and its gods.

4

Celebrating a New Social Order

Polishing the glass cases

The church seems to have almost an obsession with meetings, which I suppose is an occupational hazard when the nature of our faith requires the regular gathering together of its people. Yet it seems that so many of our meetings are designed to *prevent* us from actually meeting one another, beyond a polite hello and moderate physical proximity. I have often sat in services observing the way in which we scatter ourselves around the chairs or pews in an apparent attempt to keep a distance of at least six feet between each individual or bunch of friends.

At times I have found no difficulty in imagining each worshipper enclosed in a glass case, oblivious of the personal dramas, tragedies or joys of the other people around. Indeed, the introduction of such glass cases would in many cases be a more logical extension of the separatism that is habitually practised, and would make little difference to the relationships, except perhaps when it came to deciding who should keep them polished!

The armchair church

In America, the advent of the 'electronic church' now means that thousands of Christians can 'belong' to a church without ever leaving their armchairs and TV dinners, as the whole thing is piped into that shrine of isolation and privacy: the living room. There are, however, as we all know, countless local churches where, despite small congregations, members attend services for years and years without ever finding out more than the barest details about their fellow worshippers. Individualistic attitudes to Christianity have in fact permeated so deeply into our churches that to begin to talk in practical terms about the necessity to enter into a greater depth of relationship, involving the sharing of our lives, would probably be greeted with the kind of shock you would expect if someone had suggested that we should all become Buddhists, open up a casino in the vestry or set the church organ on fire.

And yet, if one of the original apostles were to get caught in an ecclesiastical time warp and land unexpectedly in one of our glass-case churches, what might he think? I strongly suspect that he would be shocked for quite a different reason, finding us as alien to his understanding of the body of Christ as we would be to his, and many of us able only to mutter a collection of half-baked ideas or excuses, based not upon the revelation of the kingdom of God through Christ, but upon our tastes, preferences and cultural orientation as English men and women.

Worship without frontiers

It seems that much of our worship has lost its most vital and life-giving quality, the thing that should set Christians apart as remarkably different from the fragmented society around us. That quality, which should be affirmed and celebrated whenever we meet, and should characterize our daily life, is what Paul describes in Colossians 3:11–17:

> Here there is no Greek or Jew, circumcised or uncircumcised, barbarian, Scythian, slave or free, but Christ is all, and is in all. Therefore, as God's chosen people, holy and dearly loved, clothe yourselves with compassion, kindness, humility, gentleness and patience. Bear with each other and forgive any grievances you may have against one another. Forgive as the Lord forgave you. And over all these virtues put on love, which binds them all together in perfect unity. Let the peace of God rule in your hearts, since as members of one body you were called to peace. And be thankful. Let the word of Christ dwell in you richly as you teach and admonish one another with all wisdom, and as you sing psalms, hymns and spiritual songs with gratitude in your hearts to God. And whatever you do, whether in word or deed, do it all in the name of the Lord Jesus, giving thanks to God the Father through him.

The segment of this passage that we would most readily associate with worship is probably the mention of singing 'psalms, hymns and spiritual songs'. But how many of us would be prepared to consider the whole of it as a description of the nature of true Christian worship? If worship is in any way a celebration or affirmation of the kingdom of God, then there is a sense in which the whole passage is about worship. When we choose to neglect or deliberately avoid the kind of relationships that we see described here, our singing may become in the ears of God little more than decibels and wasted energy. Worship is a celebration of the new kingdom, and the words we have just read go a long way to describe the nature of that kingdom. If we follow the passage through carefully, we will see the foundations upon which our worship should be built.

Here there are no nationalistic divisions; Jews are not better than Greeks; the British are not of more value than Asians, West Indians or Argentinians. Here there are no 'class' divisions based on different religious experiences, no exclusive and superior club for those baptized in the Holy Spirit, or caucus for the mutual protection of those who regard it with distaste or suspicion.

The rule of God's peace

Here there are no cultural prejudices but a desire to understand and accept those who are different; no divisions between the rich and the poor, the professional classes and manual labourers, but a sharing of wealth and resources. Here there is a place to belong, limitless compassion and patience, and forgiveness for one another when we make mistakes or do hurtful things. Here there is love that causes us to lay down our lives for one another. The inevitable product of all these things is the rule of peace, continued thankfulness and the growth of knowledge about God. In this context there is no lack of content or motivation for the singing of psalms, hymns and spiritual songs, as we celebrate a new order of social, economic and spiritual relationships lived to the glory of Jesus Christ. Our 'visiting apostle' would find himself completely at home in this environment while no doubt exhibiting a heartfelt sympathy and understanding for the problems of building and maintaining such a community!

A spectator sport?

It must be admitted in the light of this passage that the popular practice of worship has become tailored to individuality rather than community, and instead we have diplomatically learned to avoid anything that might upset the *status quo* of separation. We sit in rows facing the front of the building and stare at the back of each other's heads as if to watch a performance or a show, unable to see each other's faces even if we wanted to! When we enter the building how many of us search for either an empty area in which to be alone, a seat at the back near the emergency exit, or anywhere where we can avoid close contact with fellow believers we don't like or just don't know? We have loud organs playing that can be a substitute for enthusiastic singing, helping us to forget how few of us are really there! The existence of ordained professional clergymen can often create the sense of a hierarchy of spirituality, with the ordinary believer feeling that he has nothing of value to contribute, particularly if the professionals appear to run a monopoly on contributions. Hence he feels his duty is just to attend regularly in the privacy of his own thoughts and feelings.

New converts are frequently left to their own devices rather than being drawn into new friendships and a structure of teaching and pastoral care; it often seems that only those who already know how to stand on their own two feet survive. In recent times we have often been guilty of preaching an individualistic gospel, inviting people into a personal relationship with Jesus, forgetting to add that we should also be inviting them into a personal relationship with us. I suspect that we have suppressed this part of the gospel because of a niggling doubt that they might become disillusioned with what they would find. We have invited them to come and find 'purpose in life' or 'personal fulfilment' in Christ, neglecting to mention the call to die to self and become a servant of all, as part of a serving church.

'Being nice' to God

If we were to cut off from Christianity everything in it that challenges and offers to transform the way we treat other people, there would be almost nothing left. But in many cases this is what we have effectively done, by watering down the lifestyle described in our previous passage from Colossians to a vague philosophy of 'be nice to one another'. Watered down relationships will always result in watered down worship and end up in little more than 'being nice' to God. We cannot separate love for God from love for one another, or the way we relate to God (that is, worship) from the way we relate to one another. In 1 John 4:19–21 we read:

> We love because he first loved us. If anyone says, 'I love God', yet hates his brother, he is a liar. For anyone who does not love his brother, whom he has seen, cannot love God, whom he has not seen. And he has given us this command: Whoever loves God must also love his brother.

Right relationships

The importance of right relationships with one another as a prerequisite of worship is highlighted by Jesus himself in Matthew 5:23 and 24: 'if you are offering your gift at the altar and there remember that your brother has something against you, leave the gift there in front of the altar. First go and be reconciled to your brother; then come and offer your gift.' It is clear from these words that worship cannot be compartmentalized and detached from the way in which we treat people. These verses come in the context of three whole chapters of Jesus' teaching on relationships, beginning in chapter 5 with the Beatitudes, and the sheer volume of such teaching should encourage us to take verses 23 and 24 particularly seriously.

Who makes the first move?

Looking at these verses more closely, it might be easy to miss the fact that the situation cited by Jesus is one in which someone has something 'against you'. This must include situations where we ourselves may be in the right, quite innocent of sin against our brother, yet nevertheless an onus is put on the innocent party to 'go and be reconciled'. How much more then, one might ask, should the guilty party take heed of this command?

To me, this teaching suggests a refreshingly different attitude to blame, namely that as members of Christ's body, the innocent member cannot detach himself from the guilty member just because of the rights and wrongs of a situation, but shares a responsibility to make the move towards reconciliation in order that the body should be whole in every part. It is the same principle that resulted in Jesus, the only perfectly innocent man to have ever lived, making the first move towards guilty men, and even going as far as to take responsibility for our sins by dying on the cross. We must also remind ourselves that he did not come condemning, but with humility!

Right relationships release worship

How often, I wonder, do we struggle to get our worship 'off the ground' when the real reason for the absence of a sense of joy and freedom is that too many people are bringing their gifts of praise, or money, or service, to the 'altar' while making no effort to be reconciled with their fellow worshippers. When we consider that our 'altar' speaks of the place where the innocent blood of the Lamb of God was shed for the forgiveness of the guilty, then we should take special care to check that we are not coming in blatant contradiction of what that shed blood signifies. Rather, we should be reminded of Jesus' command to:

'Love one another *as I have loved you*' (my italics).

The practice of these teachings has been a transforming influence in many churches, and in opening the sluice-gates as far as worship is concerned. I have frequently witnessed meetings where the Spirit has moved the leaders to encourage reconciliation 'on the spot', often as a prelude to sharing the bread and wine of the Eucharist together. At the small cost of sacrificing natural reserved-ness, and the higher cost of sacrificing pride and fear, such breaking of barriers and healing of rifts has often come to the extent that it seemed like a dark cloud had been blown away between earth and heaven. It must be said that these were often 'crisis' occasions, and would not have been necessary had the practice of reconciliation been a normal part of the daily life of the fellowships concerned. I some-times wonder what freedom there might be in a fellowship where everybody had learned to get right with each other as a regular personal discipline, such that they always came together united; worshipping, as it were, under a clear sky rather than under a cloud.

An eternal triangle

Reconciliation is of course a positive solution for those times when the negative side of our fallen humanity has reared its ugly head, and because of our weaknesses it will continue to be a regular necessity this side of heaven. However, we are not meant to become absorbed exclu-sively in corrective measures and if we can learn to worship as the body of Christ in positive, creative ways, then a whole new realm of mutual encouragement and spiritual power will open up for us. Whereas the popular practice of worship tends towards the vertical, that is, the individual to God, the New Testament clearly shows us two directions: vertical and horizontal, towards God and towards one another. In Ephesians 5:19 we read: 'Speak to one another with psalms, hymns and spiritual songs. Sing and make music in your heart to the Lord.' As we meet together we should find ourselves in a kind of invisible triangle, joined by the Spirit and relating together in a common experience of worship yet focused upon the Lord. As we move from the horizontal plane closer to the apex of the triangle, we find ourselves moving closer together.

Singing to one another

In the light of this, we would do well to question the standard poses we adopt of closed eyes, or gazing into the middle distance, and serried ranks facing the hats and hairstyles in front. How many of us conduct conversations in this manner, even with strangers! In normal life it would be regarded as quite rude! There must be a case here for our times of worship to involve at least in part the opportunity for eye to eye contact, and the use of psalms, hymns and spiritual songs as direct exhortations to one another. It is curious how we regularly sing words that are clearly designed for encouraging others, as if they were for the Lord! How ridiculous it is when we lift our eyes and our hands heavenward and sing, 'Seek ye first the kingdom of God and his righteousness'—as if it is *God* who needs reminding!

Strengthening one another

In 1 Corinthians 14 Paul is dealing with matters of order in corporate worship, and it is clear that the pattern was not one of a majority of passive observers seeking personal spiritual enrichment from a select group of 'performers' at the front. In verse 26 we read:

> What then shall we say, brothers? When you come together, everyone has a hymn, or a word of instruction, a revelation, a tongue or an interpretation. All of these must be done for the strengthening of the church.

This must of course be seen in the context of Paul's teaching elsewhere on authority and leadership, and not mistaken as a licence for anybody to 'do their thing' without being accountable. The list of contributions is obviously a short list, a sample, and elsewhere in the New Testament numerous additional ways of contributing are mentioned. The contributions that may be brought are clearly for a specific purpose: 'the strengthening of the church'.

Coming to give

We see here a very different attitude towards our coming together, that of coming to *give*, rather than coming to *get*. In fact, the overriding difficulty for those who fill the pews rather than the pulpit is that they are rarely given an alternative to 'taking' because of the way our services are normally structured, and it requires a considerable degree of self-discipline, initiative and imagination to give to others in these circumstances. We should not, however, use such a situation as an excuse to 'cop out' but, despite the *status quo*, use self-discipline, initiative and imagination in order to find ways to build each other up. More of that, however, in Chapter 15.

'Free' worship is not cheap

There is a great deal of fear and reticence among many church leaders when it comes to putting participation into practice, and it is understandable when you have experienced the mish-mash of good, bad and indifferent contributions that can emerge when a congregation is let loose! What about the danger of certain dominant personalities trying to take over; misguided or unbalanced persons leading the meeting off into confusion; 'super-spiritual' members mistaking a vivid imagination for visions or prophecies, an individual with an 'axe to grind' using the gathering as a platform for his or her own opinions, grievances or heresies? There is no escaping the realities of these dangers, but surely it is no answer deliberately to repress such problems or pretend they are not there. Could it not be seen as facing the reality of where people are 'at', instead of running away from it? If we are scared of what our brothers and sisters might do if given the freedom to express themselves, then would it not be better to venture on to the dangerous road towards reality, renewal and change, than to go on pretending we are functioning as the many membered body of Christ?

A foundation of love and trust

Do we love and trust one another enough to be honest when your or my contribution is not helpful, or badly timed, or insensitive to the feelings of others? The answer may well be 'no', but if it is, can we not commit ourselves to loving honesty, and agree to be real with each other for the sake of the health of the whole body? Paul says in his letter to the Romans, 15:5–7:

> May the God who gives endurance and encouragement give you a spirit of unity among yourselves as you follow Christ Jesus, so that with one heart and mouth you may glorify the God and Father of our Lord Jesus Christ. Accept one another, then, just as Christ accepted you, in order to bring praise to God.

The heart behind the song

It is not the noise of our songs that brings praise and glory to the Lord. Besides, he already has an infinitely superior quality of music and song to enjoy, performed by countless angels who are no doubt extraordinarily skilled in heavenly melody such as would make our best anthems sound like funeral dirges! Instead he looks for the 'spirit of unity', the 'one heart', the attitude of accepting one another, that fuels our worship and animates our voices and bodies; he searches for the motivation of our actions and is not fooled when we try to substitute beautiful music for beautiful relationships. It may seem strange to our minds to think in terms of glorifying God with our relationships, but I would suggest that this kind of praise far exceeds the value of music, singing and dancing in the context of wrong relationships. It would be quite correct to announce in a meeting 'Let's praise the Lord' and then proceed to minister to one another's needs without a note being sung. I could guarantee, however, that if real Christ-like love was being practised, it would not be long before the praise became vocal as well!

Serving one another in worship

The attitude that Paul is exhorting the Roman church to display is that of serving others, and servanthood is surely one of the qualities most lacking in our worship. We should come together with each individual having determined in his heart to bring something that will build up someone else, hence in 1 Corinthians 14:26; 'everyone has a hymn, or a word of instruction, a revelation, a tongue or an interpretation'. We are so conditioned to meeting together for selfish benefit that even when we do make a contribution, many of us (and I freely confess to this fault) are more likely to ask ourselves 'How did I do? Were they impressed?' than to have a genuine concern for whether someone else was helped, encouraged or enlightened! When preparing to take part in a meeting, I find I have to make a deliberate effort to pray for the people who will be there, otherwise even my prayers will centre far too much upon performing well and preventing making a fool of myself—thus losing spiritual credibility!

A cure for the insecure

We may never entirely escape from the temptation towards these ego-centred thoughts and feelings, but at least we can avoid indulging them by deliberately turning our attention to the well-being of others. It is also worth remembering that such self-centredness is usually based upon insecurity—in other words, we don't feel safe with one another and are scared of rejection, failure or censure. The antidote to fear is love and I doubt if any of us will ever rid ourselves totally of feelings of insecurity, and the overconcern with self that it creates, without the depth of love and acceptance among our brothers and sisters in the church that is clearly God's desire for us.

Servants for the world's sake

Chapter 15 of Romans goes on to speak of Christ's servanthood, and attaches to it an important consquence:

> For I tell you that Christ has become a servant of the Jews on behalf of God's truth, to confirm the promises made to the patriarchs so that the Gentiles may glorify God for his mercy, as it is written: 'Therefore I will praise you among the Gentiles; I will sing hymns to your name.' Again, it says, 'Rejoice, O Gentiles, with his people' (vv.8–10).

Jesus became a servant in order to lead people from every nation to worship the one true God. The picture of the suffering servant in Isaiah 52 and 53, which emerges as a prophetic foreshadowing of Christ, comes vividly to life in the New Testament as we look at the attitudes that Jesus displayed and the life that he lived.

When Jesus commanded his followers to love one another in the way that he loved them, he effectively passed on the mission of the suffering servant to the church to be continued. Why then is servanthood connected in this passage with the Gentiles, the 'outsiders', rejoicing and singing praises (v.11)? Is it solely because of the amazing example of God's love in the servant attitude of the historical Jesus? If so, how could the Gentiles be expected to see it in the first place in order to react to it, when they were geographically and culturally so far from Judea? Would they be convinced just by verbal reports, or might they need a living flesh and blood example before the smallest note of praise left their cynical lips?

As Paul is so obviously presenting the servanthood of Jesus as an example to be followed in the church as we live and worship together, could it not be concluded that it is the living, flesh and blood demonstration of servanthood in the church that brings the reality of Christ to the Gentiles, the outsiders to faith in God, such that they praise him?

The miracle of unity

There is nothing in a divided, fragmented and violent world that can impress as much as the bringing together in love, unity, joy and celebration, of people who were once bitterly divided by economic differences, class, race, colour, ideology, culture, religion and nationality. This unity is the one thing that the world cannot achieve, and it is the lack of it that threatens our peace and, in a nuclear age, our very existence. No wonder it is remarkable enough to make 'the Gentiles' praise God! It should be obvious then that it is impossible to detach servanthood in our worship together from servanthood in our lives together, and that when these two are working together, it begins to affect the world around us. There is a rare and special quality of witness in a community of servants, worshipping a God who became a man in order to serve, and reaching out in the power of that God to serve the world. Hence there is an extension of the horizontal thrust of worship out through the church into the world.

The face of the outsider

One of the most serious dangers that we encounter when we seek to enrich our worship is our capacity as human beings to turn even the most Godward activity into a selfish pursuit. I doubt if any of us would do this deliberately, but many of us have caught ourselves in the process of carving a place for ourselves and our gifts, accompanied by a diminishing regard for serving others, and a growing sense of thirst for power or success. On a corporate level, it is possible to become so caught up in the pursuit of better, freer, richer and more creative worship that we have no time or energy left for the world outside.

Worship should not only point us to God and one another, it should also point us to the millions who have never met Jesus, and whom God loves just as much as he loves us. If indeed our worship does hide us away from the faces of the 'outsiders', I question whether we are still worshipping in reality, and whether we have in fact hidden ourselves away from the face of Jesus. True worship reveals to us the 'face' of Jesus. It is an encounter with a

Person who feels, knows, speaks and reveals himself among us as we worship ('where two or three are gathered...' (Mt 18:20)). If we are encountering in the Spirit the real Jesus, and not a distorted vision of him, then we are encountering an 'outsider'.

No exclusive elite

If Jesus in his incarnation had taken the attitude of an exclusive elite, one of a privileged few, then all of us would still be bound for hell. If he had shut himself away in order to pursue the unimaginable glory of his own relationship with his Father, then the whole of humanity would remain damned to this day. The grace of God is such, however, that he took on a very different attitude. We read in Philippians 2:5–7:

> Your attitude should be the same as that of Christ Jesus; Who, being in very nature God, did not consider equality with God something to be grasped, but made himself nothing, taking the very nature of a servant, being made in human likeness.

Jesus became an outsider, a human being in the lower social orders, despised and rejected for mixing with prostitutes and sinners. He became identified in every way but sin with a world of outsiders. How then can we build around him an exclusive club, even for his praise and worship?

The stranger outside the door

In the face of Jesus we should see the face of every outsider, particularly those who are shut out of enjoying the bare necessities of natural life, let alone spiritual life. There is one particular passage in the Bible that for me is probably the most sobering and disturbing of all—Matthew 25 where Jesus talks about when he will appear in glory to judge us:

> Then he will say to those on his left, 'Depart from me, you who are cursed, into the eternal fire prepared for the devil and his angels. For I was hungry and you gave me nothing to eat, I was thirsty and you gave me nothing to drink, I was a stranger and you did not invite me in, I needed clothes and you did not clothe me, I was sick and in prison and you did not look after me.' They also will answer, 'Lord, when did we see you hungry or thirsty or a stranger or needing clothes or sick or in prison, and did not help you?' He will reply, 'I tell you the truth, whatever you did not do for one of the least of these, you did not do it for me.' Then they will go away to eternal punishment, but the righteous to eternal life (vv. 41–46).

Our worship should reveal to us the Jesus who suffers with the poor, the hungry, the sick, the naked and the imprisoned, and our meeting with him in the Spirit should send us out to meet him in the flesh of the world's outsiders. It is so much easier and more attractive to spiritualize our worship to the exclusion of the world outside, but we must face the fact that by so doing we shut Jesus out as well.

Note: The subject of unity and shared lives has been written about extensively in recent times, and it will undoubtedly be easier to grasp the implications it throws up for the way we worship if we first understand something of what the Bible teaches about the body of Christ. Hence I am taking a risk by isolating a discussion of communal worship from the wider issues, but hope that those with a deep concern for worship already have studied, or will make it their business to, what has been written by others on the subject of unity out of deep and sometimes painful experience.

5

A Royal Invitation

Being an Englishman, and living in England, I have a deeply ingrained habit that has dominated an area of my life for nearly all my adult years. I drive my car on the left-hand side of the road. Although I rarely think of it as such, it happens to be a legal requirement in this country. Obedience to it, however, is really extremely easy, such that I don't even think to feel proud of myself when I pass a police car, and would never for one moment find myself smiling broadly at the occupants as if to say, 'Aren't I doing well, still on the left!' Such a law seems so right, and reasonable, and common sense, that we hardly think of it as a law at all, and the idea of it being burdensome is ridiculous. In fact laws like that add considerably to the overall pleasure, not to mention the safety, of motoring!

God's laws and principles are like that. They are for our own safety and enjoyment and are restrictive only in the sense that they restrict chaos, unhappiness and misery. Having looked at the way in which praise and worship overflow naturally from lives that are presented to God, bringing pleasure to both God and man, it would be incomplete if we did not consider the fact that it is also a 'legal requirement'.

Worship is not optional

I don't know if anybody has ever counted the number of
commands to praise and worship in the Bible, but even a
brief search will reveal so many of them that we must
conclude that God really does require it! Looking through
the Old and New Testament there are commands to praise,
glorify, sing praises, shout, bless, give thanks, bow down,
kneel before, offer, sing a new song to, rejoice, honour,
offer sacrifices, exalt, fear, adore, serve, extol, magnify
and many others too, and in such proportions that we
cannot treat the subject in any way as an optional extra.

Consider for example these words to the people of God
from 2 Kings 17:35–36:

> When the Lord made a covenant with the Israelites, he
> commanded them: 'Do not worship any other gods or bow
> down to them, serve them or sacrifice to them. But the Lord,
> who brought you up out of Egypt with mighty power and
> oustretched arm, is the one you must worship. To him you
> shall bow down and to him offer sacrifices...'

Worship is our destination

Even if we were to exhaust these direct commands, we
would still have to take notice of the way in which God's
absolute right to our worship is implicit throughout the
Bible. It in fact begins and ends in worship, and the whole
history of redemption of which it tells is the restoration of
mankind after he ruins everything by transferring his
worship away from his Creator to himself. The serpent's
temptation was that if Adam and Eve ate of the forbidden
fruit, they would be 'like God', and so they traded their
worship and obedience to him for the chance to be as
important as he is. In that instant, they set their own egos
up as objects of worship, their own wills over his will, and

exchanged the true worship of God for a lie. The final book of the Bible, the book of Revelation, describes the destruction of sin and evil, and ends the story with a great feast, fantastic celebrations and stupendous worship by men and angels that will characterize eternity. We catch a glimpse of perfection where everything that exists gives praise to God. If we wish to be a part of this cosmic plan of redemption, then we must add our voices to the song that God commands all his creatures to sing. And burdensome it is not!

Yes you will! No I won't!

Our social experience of receiving commands, however, may cause us some problems when we encounter God's commands. The problem is this: living as we do as part of a corrupt society, made up of sinful people, the orders we are given inevitably come from people with anything ranging from true integrity to deliberate evil intent. We learn to be suspicious, to question, to rebel and to be cynical. Sometimes we even have to disobey orders on moral grounds. Such is the condition of man that we find it difficult to trust completely those in authority over us.

Sadly, we unconsciously transfer many of these doubts and suspicions to God, and impose our experience of human authority figures on to him. This is understandable, and it is wonderful to be able to remind ourselves that Jesus understands this and himself pleads our case before the Father, as one who has lived in human society in all its corruption and distortion of the truth.

Did God really say so?

However, there is also a most insidious characteristic within us that makes us coldly resistant to God's commands. It is the very same attitude that the devil planted into Eve's mind in the Garden of Eden: '*Did* God really say?' The devil went on from planting doubt about what God had said, to blatantly contradicting it and implying that God had lied. In this way God's command was undermined, then disobeyed, and thereafter there has been, mixed like a dark evil poison into the heart of mankind, this attitude: 'Did God really say that?... Take no notice, his commands are restrictive.' We would do well to give no time to discuss or argue with this attitude when it rears its serpent head inside us, but to tread it instantly underfoot, in case we should in discussing lies find ourselves in conversation with the father of lies.

God's commands are good for us

Despite our natural wariness of human commands, there are many which, though they are commands, come to us more in the manner of an invitation. Commands like 'Come and sit up, dinner's ready!' or 'Go to my wallet and take twenty pounds for yourself' are most welcome! Without the command, the person receiving the order would clearly be the loser. This is, I believe, akin to the nature of God's numerous commands to praise and worship him. The weakness of these illustrations of course is the emphasis on coming to receive, rather than coming to give. We are indeed invited to come and get, but we must remember that it is a relationship that we are invited into—a relationship of reciprocal giving and receiving.

It may be appropriate to illustrate this by what happens when a husband or wife says to their partner: 'Come and give me a hug.' In giving a hug, you inevitably get one! Jesus said that there is more happiness in giving than there is in receiving, so when God invites us, or commands us, to worship him, he knows that in giving ourselves in this way we will also receive, and then much more than if we came with the sole intention of getting.

RSVP

Though I don't have much personal contact with the British Royal family (well, none at all actually), I have a pretty good idea about the nature of the invitation cards bearing the address of Buckingham Palace. If Her Royal Highness Queen Elizabeth II requests the pleasure of your company, you'd better be there! In fact, royal invitations historically use the term 'commands your presence', and any suggestion of it being a take it or leave it request is just not in it! Imagine this kind of invitation in the days when the monarchy ruled supreme, when heads that caused royal displeasure tended to roll! Yet we have a standing invitation from the Kings of kings, the mighty and majestic Lord of the universe, to enter into his courts with praise. How incredibly presumptuous and foolish we are if we carelessly ignore such an invitation. His invitation cards, written with a nail-pierced hand, are scattered throughout the Scriptures, and when he invites us to come, we'd better be there!

The Creator God would be perfectly within his rights to require our worship, even if he was a tyrant and not the loving Father that he is revealed to be through Christ. Indeed, the revelation of Yahweh through the Jewish nation and Christ himself shows him to be unique when compared with all human concepts of God and gods. The gods of human imagination and demonic invention appear mostly to demand worship by way of fear and threats. In primitive times and even more recent history, such abhorrent practices as child sacrifice have been regarded as necessary to appease their anger, and countless people have lived in mental, spiritual and even physical bondage trying not to anger their particular god or gods.

He is worthy of our worship

One of the marvellous truths, however, about the one
true God who has been revealed to us through Jesus is
this: he is totally and utterly worthy of our worship. He
doesn't just invite or demand it, he is worth it, with a
worthiness that will absorb our wondering minds for
eternity. One of the songs in Revelation 5 concentrates on
this facet of God the Son, revealed there as a Lamb
looking as if it had been killed:

> You are worthy to take the scroll and to open its seals,
> because you were slain, and with your blood you purchased
> men for God from every tribe and language and people and
> nation. You have made them to be a kingdom and priests to
> serve our God, and they will reign on the earth (vv. 9–10).

The song continues:

> In a loud voice they sang 'Worthy is the Lamb, who was slain,
> to receive power and wealth and wisdom and strength and
> honour and glory and praise!' (5:12).

Praise is really quite a natural thing for us to do when we
feel that someone is worthy of it. I read in a newspaper
recently the following headline: 'Praise for man who saved
girl from seal.' The man's action, his courage and his
willingness to risk his own life to save the girl, made him
worthy of praise, and no one of a healthy disposition
would deny it to him.

To attempt to expand on the worthiness of God in any
adequate way, would be to begin a whole book, and I am
sure that my lifetime would not provide enough time to
finish it. There is a very real sense in which this is the

purpose of our lives anyway, our very life and being reading like a book about the value of our Creator.

With a God like this, how can we keep quiet?

We do see, however, in this song of heaven, a focus on some of the reasons why he is so worthy. The first reason is: 'because you were slain'. We may be so familiar with the story of God's redemption of mankind that it is easy to take for granted what is an incredible divine act of grace and humility, namely that described so vividly by Paul in Philippians 2:5–8:

> Your attitude should be the same as that of Christ Jesus; Who, being in very nature God, did not consider equality with God something to be grasped, but made himself nothing, taking the very nature of a servant, being made in human likeness. And being found in appearance as a man, he humbled himself and became obedient to death—even death on a cross!

Don't you think that a God like that is worth praising!

The second reason for his supreme worth is this: 'and with your blood you purchased men for God from every tribe and language and people and nation'. What a Saviour he is, paying the terrible and ultimate price for our forgiveness, despite what we really deserve. An innocent man of immeasurable worth buying back with his own blood traitors of indescribable guilt, fit only for the grim punishment-halls of hell.

Not only does he buy us back: there is a third reason for this worthiness: 'You have made them to be a kingdom, and priests to serve our God, and they will reign on the earth.' As if it wasn't enough to take on human flesh and offer it as a sacrifice for our forgiveness, he goes on to elevate these rescued rebels to a lofty and noble status, not only to be kings and priests and reign on the earth, but as such, to engage in the highest of all acts of service, to serve God himself for ever! To quote Paul E. Billheimer (*Destined for the Throne*, Christian Literature Crusade, page 37):

> As sons of God, begotten by him, incorporating into their fundamental being and nature the very 'genes' of God, they rank above all other created beings and are elevated to the most sublime height possible short of becoming members of the Trinity itself. Although Christ is the unique and only begotten Eternal Son, yet he does not retain his glory for himself alone for he has declared, 'the glory which thou gavest me, I have given them' (Jn 17:22). Therefore, the redeemed will share his glory, his rulership, and his dominion as truly responsible princes of the Realm.

These truths, when we even just begin to comprehend them, surely leave us breathless, but when we get our breath back, how can we help but fill our lungs with air and speak, sing or shout praise to the utter worthiness of this amazing Saviour! How casual and conservative we so often are in our response to such magnificent love, to such inestimable worth!

Commands for our weaknesses

In the face of this kind of grace, you could argue: 'Who needs commands to praise him? Just try to keep me quiet!' Yet God understands us far more than we sometimes give him credit for, and he knows the weakness of our faulty and flawed personalities. He understands how easily we lose sight of him and his worthiness, how suddenly we become absorbed and distracted by the worries and troubles of life. He knows how often we entertain doubts, or lose heart in the face of adversity. For these very practical reasons he *commands* us to praise him. In fact the activity most likely to bring to vibrant life our vision of a praiseworthy God, is praise itself. It is often true that until we begin to praise, our thoughts are far away and devoid of any sense of God, but as we obey the command to praise, our spirits are stirred and begin to cut through the jungle of our tangled thoughts and feelings, and before long we break out on to a highway leading into the presence of God. God commands us to praise not only because it is his right, not only because he is worth it, but also because we often need a command to get us started at all!

God is always worth praising

Commands to praise and reasons to praise usually come together, for example in the shortest psalm, number 117— 'Praise the Lord, all you nations; extol him, all you peoples. For great is his love towards us, and the faithfulness of the Lord endures for ever. Praise the Lord.' God never leaves us for one moment without a reason to praise him. Even if we were to find ourselves with no prayers apparently answered, no good things to enjoy and give thanks for, the joys of life stolen away from us, yet his unchanging character, his faithfulness and love would still provide good enough reasons to give him the best our hearts can offer. His command is an invitation, his invitation affords us entrance into his presence, and in his presence we find an infinite number of good reasons to praise him. As David asserts in Psalm 16:11—'you will fill me with joy in your presence, with eternal pleasures at your right hand.'

6

Wired for Worship

(1) Worshipping the Father

Who are the 'true worshippers'?

'Yet a time is coming and has now come when the true worshippers will worship the Father in spirit and truth, for they are the kind of worshippers the Father seeks. God is spirit, and his worshippers must worship in spirit and in truth' (Jn 4:23, 24).

This conversation between Jesus and the Samaritan woman at a hot dirty well-side by the town of Sychar contains what is probably Jesus' most important statement on what true worship is. There is no vagueness in his words, no hint that we can worship in whatever way feels right to each one of us, but rather a clear decisive statement of the three essentials that separate those whom God declares to be 'true worshippers' from everybody else.

First, then, what constitutes a 'true worshipper'? The background to Jesus' conversation in John 4 was the old religious controversy between the Jews and the Samaritans concerning where God should be worshipped. The issue was a geographical one; should God be worshipped in Jerusalem as the Jews insisted or on Mount Gerizim as the Samaritans did? The question was to do with the externals of worship, implying location, ritual, tradition and creed.

Jesus' answer swept all these considerations aside and centred on the essential heart of worship, namely *who* we are worshipping, our relationship to him and how we are able to make and sustain a real, actual and personal approach to him. According to Jesus' words, those who would be true worshippers depend on three connections being established with God: worshipping 'the Father', worshipping 'in spirit' and worshipping 'in truth'. It may be helpful to picture these as the three pins of an electrical plug. When the three pins of the plug connect to the three corresponding holes in the socket, the circuit becomes 'live' and power can flow. Likewise it is necessary for us to be 'connected' to God in these three areas before worship becomes real. In this chapter, and the two following, we shall be looking at each of these three essentials.

Worshipping the Father

If those of you who have as yet escaped the joys of parenthood will bear with me for a moment, I will briefly indulge myself in one of its most pleasant aspects. In our family (wife, three daughters and a dog at the time of writing!), we do not hesitate to express verbally our love for one another. I must admit that for some reason, probably rooted in British reserve, the first few times I told my eldest daughter this fact, even though she was barely old enough to understand, I was slightly embarrassed. Thankfully, it quickly became quite natural, and I have been rewarded on occasions when, quite spontaneously, she has suddenly jumped on my lap and put her arms round my neck or run and hugged my leg and said, 'Daddy, I love you.' The added joy of this has been that it has always been unrelated to a request for sweets, a ride on the swing or anything else that suggests a mixed motive!

It is hard to explain exactly the effect this has on fathers, but it tends to evoke a certain melting of the insides and a dampness around the eyes, plus perhaps a lump in the throat. It is a deeply rewarding thing to be told, with unaffected simplicity and spontaneity, that your child loves you.

An astounding revelation

Surely this must be a small reflection of how God feels when we, his children, tell him the same thing. It was Jesus who revealed this marvellous truth about the fatherly nature of God to the world, and when we begin to appreciate what this means in terms of our relationship with him, it can have a transforming effect upon worship. In his conversation with the Samaritan woman in John 4:22, Jesus tells her that the Samaritans: 'worship what [they] do not know'. He then goes on to say something that must have sounded strange, if not preposterous, to her ears: 'Yet a time is coming and has now come when the true worshippers will worship the *Father*...' (my italics). Being a Samaritan, with Jewish blood in her veins and early Jewish history and teaching in her head, the idea of God as an intimate, personal Father could even have sounded blasphemous. Throughout his ministry, however, Jesus talked to his Father and about his Father, and when the scribes and Pharisees suspected that he was talking of Yahweh, the obvious implication that he was literally claiming to be Yahweh's Son offended their deepest sense of reverence, and constituted in their minds the capital crime of blasphemy. As scholars of the Scriptures, however, they must have had some idea of this concept, as there is a strong foreshadowing of it in the Old Testament, but a personal relationship with God such as this term suggests would have been unthinkable.

'Our Father...'

My interest in this led me to look in my concordance to discover how much the term Father, as a specific name for God, occurred in both the Old and New Testaments. In the Old Testament there are fourteen examples of God being referred to by the name of 'Father', and then not so much in the sense of a personal relationship but that of a father to the nation of Israel, but in the New Testament there are 228 examples, plus three occasions when 'Abba' is used—this being the word a child would use like our 'Dadda' or 'Daddy'. There are over one hundred occasions in the Gospel of John alone when the use of the word 'Father' appears. It was Jesus who taught his disciples to pray 'Our Father'. He himself, however, always said: 'My Father', indicating his special unique relationship as *the* Son of God. This we can understand, but to be invited into a similar personal relationship ourselves is nothing short of astounding!

'Abba Father'

It is worth looking a little more closely at this word 'Abba'. Although there are only a handful of occasions when the Aramaic word 'Abba' is directly transcribed, for example in the Garden of Gethsemane account in Mark, scholars tell us that the way in which the Greek for 'Father' or 'my Father' is used elsewhere suggests quite clearly that it was Jesus' normal practice to use 'Abba' when he spoke of or to God. It is to our minds, however, a little strange to think of Jesus calling God 'Dadda' or 'Daddy', because in our culture we generally grow out of 'childish terms' and replace them with adult ones. In Jewish homes, however, what started as a 'baby word' was not discarded when the children grew up. It would still be used even when the children had families of their own. It was very specifically a domestic and intimate term, used in the context of close family relationships, and the idea of addressing God in this way was totally out of the question.

Just imagine the wonder of those early disciples when they too were invited into the close family relationship of Jesus and his 'Abba', having heard Jesus use the term continually! The awesome, terrifying, even distant God that their ancestors had known was being reintroduced as something more. What Jesus revealed was certainly not *less* than, or other than, the Old Testament scriptures revealed, but rather a further dimension that completed the picture. The picture was of a God with a heart just like the heart of a father, when it is at its most tender, its most sensitive, its most generous, its most protective and its most forgiving.

'Family' love is at the heart of the universe

Our supreme and indeed original model of a loving relationship is that which can be glimpsed within the three Persons of the Godhead: Father, Son and Holy Spirit. It is quite correct in fact to understand the one true God as a type of family or, to put it the other way round, a family is a 'type', a model, of what God is like. In Genesis 1:26 and 27 (NASB) we read: 'Then God said, "Let Us make man in Our image, according to Our likeness".... And God created man in his own image, in the image of God he created him, male and female he created them.' When Adam alone had been created, God asserted that: 'It is not good for the man to be alone.'

My task here is not to attempt an exposition on the intrinsic nature of the triune God, but these verses should, I hope, begin to open up our understanding to the fact that God is not in his undivided self solitary and alone. Indeed it can be argued that a God who expresses himself by creating a society of people whose very nature it is to live in relationship, must have within his own nature that quality.

Altered images

We have to bear in mind of course that although we are made in the image of God, and set in families, we have fallen far from being a true reflection of God's nature and, for some, the mention of family relationships reawakes painful memories. Yet most of us have at least some concept of what they can and should be, and if we can picture for a moment the ideal of a loving, giving relationship, the joy of simply being together, the peace of perfect harmony, then we are some way towards putting our finger on the pulse of God's heartbeat.

Where did it all begin?

There is a fascinating chapter in Proverbs (8:29–31) that gives us some insight into this divine relationship, where wisdom, commonly understood as a personification of Jesus, speaks these words: 'when he marked out the foundations of the earth. Then I was the craftsman at his side. I was filled with delight day after day, rejoicing always in his presence, rejoicing in his whole world and delighting in mankind.' It is refreshing and exhilarating to discover that the source of delight and joy, praise and worship, is right in the very heart of God himself, and to marvel at the fact that we are invited into the 'family home'.

Worship is the response to a relationship

Within the circle of a truly loving family you will always find an increasing flow of thanks and praise and worship, as the worth of each member is affirmed by both words and deeds.

At the instant we put our trust in Jesus, and offered up our lives as a living sacrifice to God, we were adopted into God's family. We were introduced, not to a moody, selfish or mean tyrant, but to a perfectly loving, understanding and forgiving Father. It is as our relationship with him grows and develops, as we discover his love among our brothers and sisters, as we encounter his limitless grace and mercy, that praise and worship become an inevitable and glorious response. Worship, then, is a response to a relationship, and supremely the relationship is that of father and child.

Knowing God as Father changes us

I remember some years ago witnessing a most remarkable transformation in a particular person's life through the revelation of this very truth. This person, a young woman engaged in evangelistic work, had finally decided to be honest. We were at a conference, and the devotional atmosphere seemed to have brought her face to face with the fact that, unknown to anyone else, her life had become a complete contradiction. She privately confessed to a number of quite serious, habitual sins, which she just could not seem to shake. As a result, she had turned in on herself in guilt and confusion, and her life was devoid of any peace or joy, let alone praise and worship. There were three particular sins that gripped her. First of all, she was telling lies. If, for example, she was sitting opposite a stranger in a railway carriage and they engaged in conversation, she would begin to invent stories about herself. She would let it drop that she was the daugher of a millionaire or in some similar way attach a mystique to herself, and relate adventures that had no foundation whatsoever in her quite unremarkable background. Secondly, she had begun to steal. This generally took the form of shoplifting, and more than once she had slipped out of a record shop with an album under her coat. Thirdly, she was becoming embroiled in a romantic relationship with a married man, one of whose main attractions being that he said wonderful things about her! As she confessed these things, my mind was trying hard to identify what I felt sure must be there: some kind of root cause. Yet it was not clear what this was, and after talking for some time, and encouraging her to confess her sins and ask for forgiveness, I still had that 'unfinished feeling'. I prayed for her that God would reveal any root cause, and left it at that. As she went away I had the uncanny feeling that even the act of confession had some kind of ulterior motive.

The next day, the whole conference spent a long period in prayer and worship. All of a sudden, during a time of silence, she gasped. For all we knew at the time, she might have remembered that she'd left the gas on at home! Later on, however, she explained the interruption. Quite unexpectedly, she had had a vision. Call it a mental picture, a visual inspiration or whatever you like, but suddenly, vivid in her mind's eye, she had seen something amazing. She described the scene to me. God was enthroned in glory, and she was quite close to him and looking up into his face. He was smiling down at her in obvious delight, and she was returning a wondering gaze. The relationship represented was obvious; it was Father and daughter. Looking on, in open-mouthed wonder at this scene of mutual delight, was a crowd of people, marvelling at what they saw, remarking to one another in amazement. That was it; obviously God had decided to deal with this girl in his own way.

Six months later I happened to bump into her again, and she told me with delight that the vision had marked the end of her lies, her stealing, and her illicit relationship. How, you may wonder (if you haven't worked it out already!) did a revelation of that nature change her so much? The answer is that her real problem was to do with self-esteem. Various influences from her past had convinced her that she was worthless, a reject in spite of her many gifts and talents. Gnawing away for years at her insides, this was now playing havoc with her behaviour. In order to be 'somebody', she had invented tall stories involving noble origins and remarkable achievements. To draw attention to herself she stole, knowing that were she to be caught the scandal would make her somebody, if only in terms of infamy! Scandal was also a feature of her third sin, the illicit relationship, but probably more to the point was the fact that she found herself to be putty in the hands of somebody who flattered her. She wanted so much to be assured of her value and worth that she was prepared to enter into blatant sin upon false hopes of finding it. This was no excuse for her sins, but God in his mercy broke the fear of rejection by showing her his fatherly love, and illustrating so vividly her status as his child.

Filled with the Spirit of sonship

It is clear from Scripture that one of the specific activities of the Holy Spirit within the believer is to reveal to us the fatherhood of God. We read in Romans 8:15–16—'For you did not receive a spirit of fear that makes you a slave again to fear, but you received the Spirit of sonship. And by him we cry "*Abba*, Father". The Spirit himself testifies with our spirit that we are God's children.' Also in Galatians 4:6—'Because you are sons, God sent the Spirit of his Son into our hearts, the Spirit who calls out "*Abba*, Father".' The well-spring of worship is in relationship, and through the death, resurrection and ascension of Jesus we are qualified by faith to a relationship with God as Father. Furthermore, by the gift of the Holy Spirit planted within us, we are stirred to cry out to him like Jesus did: 'Abba, Father... not what I will, but what you will.'

Personal knowledge

How then does this knowledge of God as our Father affect our worship of him? There is of course a vast chasm between knowing about God, and knowing him in the sense of a relationship. Merely to know *about* God's fatherly nature will make very little difference at all to our worship of him, except possibly to enhance our aesthetic appreciation as we look on from a distance. It is only when we *know* him as Father, in terms of a living vital relationship, that our hearts are profoundly stirred by what we discover *about* him.

Our manner of approach to another person is determined largely by who we think they are, what we think they are like and how we think they might react to us. Similarly, our approach to God is conditioned by our concept of him, whether accurate or distorted. If we suspect that he is too busy with more important matters, as if we think there is a great queue in front of us, we won't want to bother him. If we see him as a tyrant, watching us sternly for any false moves, ready with a big stick to wallop us, we will come very warily! If, on the other hand, we see him as a soft and indulgent 'super-daddy', we may come presumptuously, blundering carelessly onto holy ground.

If, however, we know him by the revelation of the Holy Spirit and in our daily experience of him as a personal loving heavenly Father, and are acquainted with both his gentleness and his awesome holiness, we will run to him as children with open arms and yet deepest respect. The most important Person that ever existed loves you and me! The Creator of the universe has revealed himself as having the tender heart of a loving father, and has by his Spirit made us his true-born children. He knows your name, he knows my name, he laughs and weeps with us! In him we have discovered that we are valued infinitely far above our worth. How can we keep quiet about such a God?

7

Wired for Worship

(2) Worshipping in Spirit

John 4:24 'God is spirit, and his worshippers must worship in spirit....'

The meeting was not going at all well. There was an atmosphere of suspicion accompanied by a creeping paralysis of the arms, legs and jaws as I attempted to lead the people into a time of enthusiastic praise and worship. The harder I tried, the more my enthusiasm and jollity grew thin and unconvincing, and little signs of annoyance began to creep into my tone of voice. I encouraged, I explained, I joked, I gently cajoled and then finally handed over to the preacher to see how he would manage. As I sat at the front trying to adjust my facial expression to something more positive than my true feelings were suggesting, I was feeling sorely tempted to dwell on thoughts like 'pearls before swine' and 'why did I accept this invitation anyway?' Having dipped into my considerable resources of self-justification for a while, I began to be a little more objective and, I hope, compassionate towards the people who had just been subjected to my exhortations. What I decided I had been grappling with was not at heart a resistance to praising and worshipping, or even to my style of leading it, but something more basic.

Running on empty

I had been trying to draw out something that was not there, or at least present in such small quantities as to be almost negligible. They were running on 'empty'. The wells were dry and all I got was the hollow clanking of the bucket as it rattled in dry hearts. I say this not to judge them—they were probably living out of what they had been taught—but 'living waters' obviously did not feature much! I learned a lesson through this kind of experience: that praise and worship are the overflow of a way of life, of a *life* of worship, and that no amount of encouragement, enthusiasm, methodology or threats can draw true praise out of spiritually parched lives. In Matthew 12:34 Jesus is reported as saying: 'For out of the overflow of the heart the mouth speaks.' Although Jesus was at the time talking specifically about good and bad words and deeds, the principle still applies. It is the overflow of our hearts that provides the fuel for worship.

The overflow pipe

Years ago, when I lived at home with my parents, one of the houses we lived in (we lived in them one at a time I hasten to add!) had what is a common feature of many houses. On an outside wall, about twelve feet up and projecting over a concrete path, was a pipe. Attached to this pipe on the inside of the house was a bath, and this particular pipe was connected to a little hole just beneath the taps, called an overflow. This overflow hole and its connecting pipe were a dead giveaway if any of us children had, in the pursuit of swimming experience, overfilled the bath, and our guilt was yet more explicitly revealed should one of our parents or a visitor walk on the path beneath the pipe just as somebody was practising a belly-flop! Praise and worship are the overflow of a life that is filled with God, and to carry the illustration over to our bodies for a moment, our overflow hole is situated just under the nose!

It is obvious from John 4:4 that true worship can only be offered when, by the power of the Holy Spirit, our own spirit worships him. God is spirit, and we must be brought into his dimension to worship him as he requires. It was the presence of the Holy Spirit in the lives of Paul and Silas that inspired them, though badly beaten up, flogged and imprisoned in the stocks of the Philippian jail, to pray and sing hymns late into the night. This was not bravado, defiance or 'whistling in the dark', but a powerful stirring of the Spirit within them, eventually resulting in a violent earthquake and the conversion of the jailer! It is also clear from Luke 10:21 that Jesus' source of joy in worship was the Holy Spirit: 'At that time Jesus, full of joy through the Holy Spirit, said, "I praise you, Father..."'. It is wonderful to consider that the same Spirit that caused Jesus to be filled with joy as he praised and thanked his heavenly Father is in us as well.

Where the Spirit is—things happen

Wherever the Holy Spirit is mentioned in the Bible, it seems that something is happening. From the creation of the earth to the resurrection of Jesus, Pentecost and the Acts of the Apostles, he is powerfully active. If we think that all he does is to create a nice atmosphere at a meeting, we are guilty of the deepest underestimation. The Hebrew word for 'Spirit' in the Old Testament could also mean 'wind' or 'breath', but if we are thinking of soft summer breezes, we must remember that the commonest sort of wind in the Middle East was fierce, hot and often frighteningly forceful. Neither is the word for 'breath' referring to restful breathing; it was used for the fast breathing of someone in great exertion. When we enter into worship in the dimension of the spirit, we must not expect always to be wafted gently like model sailboats on a quiet pond; there is power there to blow a hurricane or send the spiritual equivalent of any number of ocean-going schooners slicing through the waves!

The dynamic behind corporate worship

Possibly the most detailed set of instructions about how Christians ought to worship is found in 1 Corinthians 12 and 14, chapters that are rich in references to, and content about, the Spirit and his workings in the gathered body of believers. We read of speaking by the Spirit of God, the manifestation of his Spirit, people being given messages through the Spirit, faith by the same Spirit, healing by that one Spirit, gifts being given to each one as the Spirit determines and so on. In chapter 14 there are numerous references to the activity of the believer's own spirit in praise, proclamation and the edification of the church. A reading of these passages makes it perfectly clear that while there were to be leaders, an exercise of self-control by all, and order as opposed to confusion, the real dynamic of the meeting was the unseen presence of the Holy Spirit pouring out the love and grace of God through the faith and love of the believers as they met to glorify him and bless one another.

Worship in the fourth dimension

What Jesus described to the woman at the well was a dimension of worship about which she had no concept. To her, worship was conducted by professionals in a certain place, at certain times, and the 'hot' issue of the day was should it be in the temple at Jerusalem or on Mount Gerizim. Jesus was announcing a new dimension and a new location. The new dimension was to be that of the spirit: 'Jesus answered, "Everyone who drinks this water will be thirsty again, but whoever drinks the water I give him will never thirst. Indeed, the water I give him will become in him a spring of water welling up to eternal life"' (Jn 4:13–14). The fresh bubbling spring water that Jesus spoke of is, of course, the Holy Spirit.

Announcing the Portatemple!

Concerning the new location of worship, Paul declares in 1 Corinthians 6:19, 'Do you not know that your body is a temple of the Holy Spirit, who is in you, whom you have received from God?' When we first trust in Christ for our salvation, we are born again by the Spirit into the dimension of the Spirit, and he takes up residence inside our bodies. True worship is a supernatural activity in a natural body. Paul speaks, in Philippians 3:3 of, 'we who worship by the Spirit of God', and again in 1 Corinthians 2:14, 'The man without the Spirit does not accept the things that come from the Spirit of God...because they are spiritually discerned.'

Until the divine Source of worship dwells within us, we cannot be the true worshippers that the Father seeks, and until that Source bubbles up and becomes a well of 'living water', we will find ourselves dry and thirsty, looking inwards at the empty void rather than upwards at the Giver. But why is it that so many Christians have been born again by the Spirit for many years and yet never known the experience of this inexhaustible supply of living waters overflowing into praise and worship?

Another unremarkable Sunday afternoon

We sat in my parents' lounge, eyes closed, praying occasionally. It was one of our prayer times, and 'we' were the five members of a musical singing group, formed for the purpose of evangelizing in church-based coffee bars. I was about seventeen or eighteen years old and, according to the spiritual *status quo* of the times, regarded as reasonably mature for my age and certainly zealous. However, we knew almost nothing about praise and worship, and the 'freest' we ever got was when in the Young People's Fellowship we would have a sing-song. This consisted of calling out the numbers of our favourite songs in the songbook and singing them one after the other, with little regard for anything except each person getting his or her favourite in before someone else suggested a song that you hated!

But back to the prayer meeting. I remember sitting there, eyes shut tight, concentrating my mind on God, thinking of some of the good things that are good to think about God! As I did, I experienced a pleasant sensation of being about ten feet tall, almost a floating feeling, such as you might get after a large Sunday dinner, sitting replete and relaxed in an armchair, drifting into a doze. You might be right in thinking that was a quite unremarkable experience. The only reason I remember it, is because at the time it was the most I had ever 'felt' in the context of praying and worshipping, and I was excited about it. It was, however, just a mental experience, on the same level as nearly all my devotional practices at that time. We knew of nothing more, and tended to assume that because our experience (or lack of it) was the 'norm', there was in fact nothing more that we could reasonably expect.

A comparatively normal Christian

If somebody was to refer to Jesus' words in John 4:24 about worshipping 'in spirit', I would assume that because I was a sound Bible-believing Christian, conformed to the norm of non-conformism, then whatever it was, I must be doing it anyway! The truth of the matter was that, though I had indeed been 'born again' by the Holy Spirit (I was five years old at the time and still remember it!), I had never been led into any kind of release of the spirit such as would create an overflow of praise and worship.

Faith comes by hearing

I have often thought about this in the light of Romans 10:17, 'faith comes from hearing, and hearing by the word of Christ'. Although I had been familiar with the story of Jesus and the Samaritan woman since my childhood, it was not until I met people who clearly experienced a new quality of life in the Spirit, and seemed to have discovered this inner source of joy and spiritual power, that I realized there was something tangible to be experienced. I was suddenly aware that, by comparison, my well was dusty and dry. When somebody preaches about or witnesses to a biblical truth that has become a dynamic part of their lives, faith seems to be generated in the listener in a special way, and this is what happened to me. I was faced with the possibility that I might have to ask God for the experience of the doctrine I knew so well.

Theory is safer

It is sad but true of so many of us that we think we have the fullness of all that the Bible teaches simply because the doctrines are familiar to us. Could it also be true that we prefer the theory to the reality, especially when the reality might involve trusting ourselves to God in areas beyond the control of the intellect, or taking the risk of being let down? The doctrines are vital, but they are there to explain, to interpret, to preserve from corruption and *to lead us into* the experience of God's promised gift of the Holy Spirit.

You mean... just ask?

God, in his grace and mercy, never demands anything from us that he does not at the same time offer to us. The passage that clinched the matter for me was Luke 11:13 where Jesus says after so clearly illustrating his point to his listeners: 'If you then, though you are evil, know how to give good gifts to your children, how much more will your Father in heaven give the Holy Spirit to those who *ask* him!' It is worth relating my experiences here, not in any way to suggest a norm (in fact it should be the opposite!), but possibly to illustrate the 'ordinariness' of something that has become in some people's minds over-dramatized, 'scary', or seemingly out of reach.

I walked down the quiet suburban street, counting off the numbers until I reached the one that corresponded to the address that I had been given. It was early summer and I had recently returned from college for the vacation; I was feeling a little melancholy. Still fresh in my mind was the disappointment of the previous few months, which had been dominated by a lengthy spiritual crisis, or rather the closest that my placid personality ever got to one! I could clearly remember standing under the stars on the college campus after a Christian meeting, so depressed by the apparent spiritual poverty I had just been an unwilling part of, that I seriously wondered whether I was just fooling myself about God.

I had started to be honest with myself, which usually brings you to the conclusion that you haven't been honest before! I had been 'witnessing' to unbelievers, but mainly on the basis of what God was doing in other people's lives. The racy Christian paperbacks of the day provided a great resource of stories and experiences, but they were not mine. I was ashamed of myself, and ashamed of my fellow Christians for the sham we seemed to be perpetuating, and yet somehow, intuitively, I felt that there must be more to Christianity than we knew. The decision I made out there under the stars (most of these type of things happen under the stars!) was that either I had to carry this new honesty about my disappointment with God to a practical withdrawal from 'hypocritical' Christian activities, or find what was missing.

I decided to find what was missing and proceeded to search the Scriptures and search for Christians who seemed to possess what I lacked. Three months later, having obtained the said address from a friend (whose life had been somewhat revolutionized through contact with the people living there), I gingerly opened the garden gate and proceeded to ring the doorbell of this strange house, wherein I had been told, a group of Spirit-filled Christians met on this particular evening, every week, and who for all I knew at that very moment might be setting up the chandeliers ready for a swinging session! To cut a long meeting short, I ended up asking for prayer to be filled with the Spirit, and with understanding and wisdom they explained certain scriptures to me and, in a separate room, two of them laid hands on me and together we simply asked our heavenly Father for his gift.

Nothing happened. I waited for the tongues of fire, the mighty rushing wind, and every time a car rushed by the window my heart jumped an inch or two as I thought, 'Here it comes!' As the minutes ticked by my temptation was to react with thoughts like 'You see, it's true, nothing will ever happen to me', and 'I guess I'm not spiritual enough yet'. But I hung on to the scriptures: '... how much more will your Father in heaven give the Holy Spirit to those who *ask* him!' I had asked. It was all I could do, except now, having asked, to trust. It was out of my hands, and into his. I went home subdued but fairly peaceful. God has a sense of humour. He also knows us inside out, and knows how sometimes our very trying, our striving too hard for experience of him makes it difficult for us to receive his gifts. Back home, everybody else had gone to bed and it was late (these charismatics have no sense of time!), and so I proceeded to the bathroom to clean my teeth and get ready for bed.

I was half-way through cleaning my teeth, quietly thanking God for hearing my prayer, but no more, when quite unexpectedly I found myself smiling. Where the smile came from I wasn't sure but there was suddenly a lot more of whatever was causing it, welling up inside! I quickly finished my teeth (still smiling and almost laughing) and adopted a more 'spiritual' pose, kneeling by the bath, but it wasn't the bath that was filling up, it was me! This was totally new, I'd never felt like this before; I was so full up with joy and peace that I spent the next hour right there, *enjoying* God for the first time in my life. I wasn't generating it, in myself I had been calm, almost melancholy, and now it was almost as if my dubious doubtful mind was looking on and saying: 'Hey, what's this! What's going on? Stop it!' But my spirit had been liberated, and I remember lying at last in my bed, the fixed grin still on my face, praising and thanking God, and gingerly trying out a new spiritual language that had presented itself to my tongue with no regard at all for the objections thrown up by my incredulous brain!

My rusty tap had at last been turned on, and what came

out was a stream of praise and worship, originating in my spirit where the Holy Spirit had found at least an open channel of faith through which to glorify my heavenly Father. Though my progress was slow, and my mistakes many, something began over that sink, toothbrush in hand, that has changed, and will continue to change, my whole life. A well of praise was opened that has never failed to satisfy my thirst when I have dipped into it.

I don't recommend *my* experience to others, because through the same truths and promises God has something special and unique for each individual. But one thing remains identical, and that is his desire that all of us should experience and enjoy everything that Jesus paid for with his blood, and one of the greatest of these things is the promise of the Holy Spirit in all his fullness, power and glory.

To worship 'in spirit' is to tap into the very source of worship himself, the inexhaustible, endlessly praising Spirit of God, and to allow him liberty to join with our own spirit in expressing through our mind and body the worth of our saviour Jesus, and the love of our heavenly Father.

'If you knew the gift of God, and who it is who says to you: "Give me a drink", you would have asked him, and he would have given you living water.'

8

Wired for Worship

(3) Worshipping in Truth

The third pin of our 'electrical plug' illustrating the essential characteristics of a true worshipper, is the pin of truth. We have seen that true worship is an actual, real approach to God. It is not dependent on being in a certain place, but on being in a certain relationship with God, that of Father and child, and being brought by faith into a certain dimension, namely that of the spirit. The third pin is equally vital despite the fact that many electrical appliances work without the earth wire connected! This would be a weakness in the illustration except for the fact that the earth connection is the one that both protects the user from harm and, in the case of radio receivers, cuts down interference from other sources. There are some parallels here that I trust will be self-evident.

Truth originates in God himself; it is an intrinsic part of his character, and therefore all his words and deeds bear the divine hallmark of truth. If our worship is to make a real live connection with this God of truth, then our lives, thought patterns and beliefs must conform to the truth about him. Any other 'pin' will not fit.

Reality versus ritual

In his conversation with the Samaritan woman, Jesus was announcing the arrival of a new age in which worship would no longer be seen to depend on buildings, holy places, ceremonies, rituals and sacrifices, but on a personal relationship with God. All those things had been symbols of what was to come, and now Jesus himself was announcing the reality of the fulfilment of all that Judaistic worship had foreshadowed. The holy of holies was no longer shut off from the common man or woman, but open to all who come by way of Jesus. Yet more astounding, he was introducing God as a personal, loving Father, and one who actively seeks worshippers.

In order to worship, this relationship with God our Father must be a reality in our lives, so that our worship is not dependent on the things that can be seen—the buildings, ceremonies, rituals and trappings of religion that can so easily become a substitute for a personal knowledge of God. Worship that depends on the externals for its existence is not real worship at all; true worship is what you have left when the externals are taken away. This does not mean that certain aids to worship are not valid and useful, but they are useless without the internal reality.

Worship in truth is worship that arises out of an actual encounter with God, a response to the experience of knowing God's real presence and activity in our daily lives. This has nothing to do with sentiment, thinking religious thoughts or having aesthetic experiences in church buildings; any religion can give you that sort of thing.

Worship in sincerity

On one occasion Jesus was challenged by some Pharisees and scribes about his disciples' failure to obey the religious traditions of the day. He answered them first by exposing the way in which they used tradition to invalidate the word of God, and then by quoting some words of Isaiah chapter 29:

> These people... honour me with their lips, but their hearts are far from me. They worship me in vain; their teachings are but rules taught by men.

This leaves no doubt that true worship must be a sincere expression of the heart if it is to be acceptable to God. In David's song of confession, Psalm 51:6, he declares: 'Surely you desire truth in the inner parts.'

Just as the lettering in sticks of seaside 'rock' goes right through from top to bottom, our lives must be internally imprinted with the character of Jesus, and not just decorated on the outside with a sticky label saying 'Christian'.

The Pharisees and scribes were concerned about conformity to external rules, by which they kept people in bondage. Jesus was concerned with the hidden places of the heart and what comes out from deep within us. Heart and lips must be in harmony if we are to worship in truth.

Worship in the light of revealed truth

Having begun by focusing on the reality of our relationship with God, and the sincerity of our hearts, we must also recognize the need for our worship to be guided by objective truth.

In the holy place of the tabernacle there was a seven-branched candlestick that was the only source of light for the priests as they worshipped. It was not natural light from the sun, but from a flame fuelled by oil. In the same way, we need to worship according to the truth revealed in the Scriptures, as it is illuminated in our hearts and minds by the supernatural light of the Holy Spirit: 'Your word is a lamp to my feet and a light for my path' (Ps 119:105). God has revealed the truth about himself in the Scriptures, culminating in the most vivid revelation of all, the person of Jesus Christ. We read in John 1:18—'No-one has ever seen God, but God the only Son, who is at the Father's side, has made him known.'

To worship in truth means to worship according to God's own revelation of himself and his purposes for mankind, and not according to the religions, philosophies, ideas and inventions of man. So we worship according to the truth about Jesus, that he is our Saviour, Prophet, Priest and King—our supreme example of manhood, and an undistorted image of the Creator. Without the knowledge and application of these and other marvellous truths about Jesus, our worship would be shrouded by mists of ignorance and uncertainty.

If reality and sincerity in worship can be likened to the love relationship at the heart of a marriage, the objective truth of the Scriptures can be likened to the legal contract of the social institution of marriage that keeps it within the right boundaries.

To this end we have the priceless gift of the Holy Spirit, whom Jesus promised in John 16:13, 'will guide you into all truth'. This truth is not a doctrinal formula to be learned, but the living word of God to be obeyed. Worship that is not illuminated, refreshed and invigorated by the truth about Jesus very soon becomes either jaded and wearisome, or frothy and unreal. Both extremes can open the door to the elevation of subjective experience above the revealed truths of the Scriptures, and lead into error.

Worship in integrity

I believe that many of us unconsciously think of worship as something we 'do' to God, a kind of broadcast we send out over the distance between earth and heaven. If we think in this way, we may go on to detach ourselves and our morality from our worship. This separation of the 'spiritual' and the 'rest' will always draw worship into unreality. The prophet Amos delivered some very hard words from the Lord to people who tried to detach their worship from their behaviour:

> I hate, I despise your religious feasts; I cannot stand your assemblies.... Away with the noise of your songs! I will not listen to the music of your harps. But let justice roll on like a river, righteousness like a never-failing stream! (5:21–24)

The absence of justice and righteousness and the presence of idolatry in their lives cancelled out the validity of their worship, reducing it to a meaningless noise in the ears of God. There was no doubt that they were continuing the outward form of religion, probably with enthusiasm and cultural richness, but because of its lack of moral integrity it brought God's judgement not his blessing. I wonder how many of us have stood up with the congregation to sing, give thanks and worship, and then gone back to our family relationships, our business practices and social lives and failed to purge out our own injustices, sins and idolatries. To worship in truth is to stand before God with the words on our lips matching the actions in our lives, living a life in which belief and behaviour are integrated.

Anyone who is foolish and careless with live electrical wiring runs the risk of death or injury. Similarly, we must remember that 'our God is a consuming fire' (Heb 12:29) and we disregard his call to worship with integrity at our peril.

Truth in character

I began this chapter by reminding us that truth originates in the character of God, and all his words of truth and deeds of truth flow out from who he is. In his grace, he is redeeming us back from the moral corruption, lies and distortions of a fallen world, to make us into 'true' people, accurately reflecting his character. Truth in character bears the hallmarks of honesty, reliability, faithfulness, consistency and, above all, love, and these qualities are surely ones that God desires to see flowing out in the way we worship him.

9

Worship and Wholeness

The body in question

Under the orange and blue striped canvas of the enormous marquee, another celebration and teaching evening was in full swing. The sense of God's presence was giving rise to praise of a very enthusiastic nature, there were smiles everywhere, voices rang out, arms were raised, hands were clapped and even some legs got liberated and danced for joy. In the midst of one such group of worshippers sat a severely disabled Christian man in an invalid 'buggy'. No one would have blamed him for feeling depressed or resentful at those around him who were praising God with agile and healthy bodies, while he could not even stand up. No one would have blamed him for excusing himself from the meeting and trundling off in his electric buggy out into the windy night and back to his room. Apparently nothing of the kind even entered his head, because as the spirit of praise grew stronger those nearby were treated to a lovely example of selfless praise. The buggy was well equipped for street use, and there he sat, flashing head-lights, stop lights, indicator lights, warning lights, in fact anything that flashed, moved or made a sound was in use as he gave all he had got in praise to the Lord he loved! I would not be at all surprised if, as God received and enjoyed his gift of worship that night, this man's expression was the most precious offering. Like the widow's mite, he had very little in human terms to give, but he gave more than anybody else because it was everything he had.

What a rebuke this was to those of us with healthy bodies knowing that we often give so little to God in praise, acting as observers rather than participants, neglecting to employ our whole being to show how much we reckon him to be worth. But how far should we go in physical expressions of worship? Is hand-raising and dancing just a passing fad, is it not irreverent and disorderly, or just something for those of us with extrovert personalities? In fact, these kind of questions are part of a much bigger issue, and many of them get answered when we understand something of the influences that have formed our thinking.

Plato rules OK!

Sadly it is true that in every age, including our own, the church has imbibed much of the world's philosophy, even when it directly contradicts the teaching of its Hebrew-Christian roots, and so it is important to see how our own thinking may have been distorted in this respect.

Plato, the Greek philosopher, headed a school of thought that preached that human beings were a unity of two parts, soul and body, but that the soul was superior to the body. This is generally termed 'Platonic dualism', and led to religious attitudes and practices that would attempt to subserve and negate the body in favour of the soul, and regard the body as evil—or at least a serious danger to religious purity. However, if we look right back to the roots of the Christian view of man, namely to the revelation that came through the Hebrew race from its earliest days, we will see quite a different view. In historic Hebrew belief and culture there is no false division made between the spiritual and the physical, no dividing up into different parts of differing values, no 'disembodying' of belief; in fact, quite the reverse is nearer to the truth.

A human trinity

The Bible's teaching is that we are tripartite beings, comprised of spirit, soul and body. (See 1 Thess 5:23; Lk 1:46; Heb 4:12.) We can identify our component parts, but for the purposes of our earthly existence we are clearly a unity of inextricably interwoven parts, evidenced by the fact that any attempt to separate mind from body, or spirit from mind, would be to pronounce a literal sentence of death! Yet living as we do in a world divided and distorted by sin, where the truth about the nature of being human has in many respects been replaced by lies or half-truths, we often find within ourselves unhealthy tensions that work against true peace of body, mind and spirit, and against peace between these members of our human trinity. If we are to worship with our whole being we must recover an understanding of God's perspective on what constitutes a whole human being.

It is highly significant that in the Hebrew language words that we translate and popularly interpret as representing something exclusively 'spiritual' nearly always carry a parallel physical meaning. For example, the various words that we translate as 'worship' indicate also a variety of physical attitudes. In John 4:16–24 the word repeatedly used for worship carries the various meaning of to kiss, bow down, and prostrate oneself. Elsewhere the word is literally 'to serve' or 'to minister', indicating actions that involve the unified commitment of the whole person, body, mind and spirit.

The division of sacred and secular

There has continued into recent times a popular but insidious belief that life can be successfully compartmentalized, particularly into the religious and the secular. This has been, for millions of nominal Christians, a convenient way of escaping the practical demands of Christ's teaching. To achieve this, one simply labels religion as 'private' and 'too personal to be talked about', and concentrates on preserving the traditional, cultural and artistic heritage of the church, not as a good and proper way of enriching living faith and worship but as a means of keeping open the door to private aesthetic experiences in church buildings. Meanwhile one's business, social and domestic life carries on according to the world's *status quo*, and avoids any challenge that 'beliefs' may present to our behaviour. In this way, an attempt is made to separate the 'sacred' and the 'secular' in a way that the Bible never does.

Here again we see the influence of Greek thought, namely the very idea that 'belief' can be detached from daily life and practice. In Hebrew understanding, the word 'belief' itself suggests not an abstract set of ideas about the way one should or might live, but rather a code of life in practice. Hence, for example, the popular statement 'I believe in God' must be critically examined in the light of the 'believer's' manner of life, and further questions asked regarding the kind of God he or she claims to believe in. A *genuine* belief in a God of judgement, for example, will result in the believer measuring his life constantly against God's standards, and adjusting it accordingly! How many of us in these terms *really* believe in a God of judgement?

Salvation is not just 'spiritual!

It has been said, and I believe quite rightly, that the only truly secular thing in the world is sin. It is of course a stark fact of this fallen world that sin has thoroughly corrupted God's perfect handiwork, but a correct reading of Scripture will show us that the gospel is a plan of redemption not only of the spiritual side of a man, but of his body and of the whole of creation. Paul instructs us in Romans 8:19–23:

> The creation waits in eager expectation for the sons of God to be revealed. For the creation was subjected to frustration, not by its own choice, but by the will of the one who subjected it, in hope that the creation itself will be liberated from the bondage to decay and brought into glorious freedom of the children of God.... Not only so, but we ourselves, who have the firstfruits of the Spirit, groan inwardly as we wait for our adoption as sons, the redemption of our bodies.

Jesus came announcing the arrival of the kingdom of God, and demonstrating the power of that kingdom over the sickness, disease, death and decay in people's bodies. Not only that, but he exercised power over the physical elements, commanding a storm at sea to cease, a fig tree to wither and the molecules in a few loaves and fishes to multiply enough to feed 5,000 hungry people. Within this cosmic plan of liberation, salvation is available to the whole person, body, mind and spirit, and we will eventually see the redemption from decay even of the planet that supports our physical existence.

A suspicion of the body

The Scriptures, consistently and refreshingly, present us with a view of man as a complete unity, with no internal ruptures between thought and action, spiritual experience and social behaviour, inward emotions and bodily expression. Where these are seen as divided in Scripture, it is usually as the result of sin. The gospel is a gospel of wholeness, where all things come together and find their unity in Christ, and not least of these is the bringing towards wholeness of the torn and scarred human personality. I believe that if we were to adopt a more biblical view (that is, God's perspective) of ourselves then we would enjoy far more not only the experience of praising God, but also the whole experience of living. The infiltration of Platonic dualism into English culture, and consequently into the church, has tended to create a suspicion of, and even a fear of, using our bodies in worship, and a subtle denial that Christianity has anything much to do with them in practice. In the majority of our churches it is still an unwritten law that for the congregation the only physical gestures permitted in worship are sitting, standing and sometimes kneeling. Any departure from this ecclesiastical protocol is likely to be the cause of quite another set of physical gestures, namely expressions of disapproval, embarrassment and shock—in fact, a most eloquent set of statements delivered in 'body language' from the rest of the congregation!

We all use body language

The fact of the matter is that in normal everyday life we speak with our bodies as much if not more than we do with our tongues. This is perfectly natural and is a part of the whole business of communication. When we are sad or upset, we want to bury our faces and weep. When we are joyful and happy, we want to dance and sing. When we are angry we become animated and agitated. The very word 'agitated' is used to describe both inward feelings and outward gestures, because they happen at the same time.

It has been known and understood for a long time, both in the commonsense teachings of most cultures and in contemporary psychiatry, that the repression of emotions, feelings and inward convictions can cause stress and tension, neurosis and even mental illness. But the wholeness that comes through Christ first heals us and then begins to release us into a worship that wells up in the spirit, is informed by the mind, and expressed through the body. It could be argued that there is no moment of more perfect unity of personality than that which comes when a person worships the Father in spirit and in truth, when the spirit is exhilarated, the mind and imagination stimulated, and the body freely expressing 'all that is within'. In King David's exhortation to himself in Psalm 103:1, he cries: 'all that is within me, bless his holy name' (AV). It is unnatural to feel deep convictions and emotions within and not to show them. Why then do we limit 'body language' to God to the equivalent of the verbal vocabulary of a parrot?

Like a little child

Much of the delightfulness of children is their naturalness and spontaneity, their lack of inhibitions and sophistication. They let you know how they feel, frequently to the embarrassment of their parents when in public places! Sometimes it seems that 'growing up' is a process of hiding our feelings, of adopting behaviour patterns that are not really comfortable but are expected of us. We develop a fear of being different, of being rejected by the majority; we force ourselves into a harness that cuts and chafes, and so, gritting our teeth, we pull our burdens of conformity throughout our lives. It is nevertheless true that for those outside the grace of God, it is better to chafe under the law than to break free into what would quickly become anarchy—everyone expressing their inward feelings of hatred, lust and covetousness without restraint! However, under the 'law of the spirit of life in Christ Jesus', the perfect law of liberty, the rule of love, would we not be vastly richer towards God and each other were we to express ourselves in the natural way that children do, as unified personalities bubbling with life and vitality? Of course, if the inward life is not there, then any attempt at rich outward expression would be meaningless and hypocritical. But if it is there, then the expression of it would confirm it, strengthen it and encourage its permeation into the whole personality. Lamentations 3:41 says: 'Let us lift up our hearts and our hands to God in heaven.' The spiritual, mental and physical are designed to function in harmony.

'Glorify God in your body'

It is worth saying a little more about the body, simply because it is mostly with our body that we have difficulties as Christian worshippers. Paul exhorts in 1 Corinthians 6:20—'Glorify God in your body' (AV). He doesn't say that we should glorify God *despite* our bodies, but *in* them. He goes on to explain why in verse 20—'For you have been bought with a price.' In some parts of the church it needs to be shouted from the rooftops that Jesus paid the ultimate price not only for our 'souls' but also for our bodies. Salvation is a complete package; it is to do with the redemption of the whole person, in fact, the whole of creation, of heaven and earth, of things spiritual and of things physical. It is not solely a spiritual salvation—it is also to do with molecules and cells!

Centuries ago, Tertullian wrote in his treatise *On The Flesh of Christ* the following words: 'Our birth he reforms from death by a heavenly regeneration; our flesh he restores from every harassing malady; when leprous, he cleanses it of stain; when blind, he rekindles its light; when palsied, he renews its strength; when possessed by devils, he exorcises it; when dead, he reanimates it—then shall we blush to own it?' (*De Carne Christi* 4). Somewhere alongside Platonic dualism there has crept into popular theology the idea that heaven is an ethereal existence of floating spirits and eery music. The Bible speaks of no such thing. Heaven is presented to us as solid and tangible, peopled by perfected saints in real spiritual bodies. Jesus was the first to be clothed in such a 'resurrection' body when he rose from the dead, and he was solid. He even ate a piece of fish to prove that he was not a ghost! He was at the same time able to enter the room without the inconvenience of doors or windows, demonstrating a fundamental development in his new material make-up! When will we get used to the idea that we are destined not for an eternity without one, but with a new one! Without our bodies, we are dead and no longer have any earthly use for our spirits and minds; it is *in* our bodies that we should glorify God, and therefore *with* our bodies that we most naturally should worship him. We look forward to a bodily resurrection, but meanwhile we enjoy the gift of a body here and now, without which we would have no touch, taste, sight, smell or hearing; no way to sense or interpret reality. In gratitude we offer it back to God as a means of serving and worshipping him, while experiencing the healing and wholeness that he brings to it as an integral part of a complete salvation.

By giving so much attention to bodily expression, I would not like to give the impression that all praise and worship meetings should be the ecclesiastical equivalent of a cup final crowd at Wembley! It is nevertheless curious how on a Saturday afternoon, many clergymen and laymen can happily function in an extraordinarily liberated physical manner on the terraces, celebrating their team's victory over another team, and then on Sunday adopt a sombre, parsonic and restrained manner when celebrating Christ's victory over the world, the flesh and the devil! Of course there should be a profound reverence in the presence of God, particularly when we remember the price of that victory, but there is also 'fullness of joy'! Although it may be true that one of our greatest needs is for richer, louder and more expressive praise, the Bible does not back up those who would swing either to an exclusive preference for silence and sobriety, or for wild enthusiasm. The fact of the matter is that the Bible makes room for everything that legitimately expresses the life and salvation God has put within us. We see there a broad spectrum from silence to dancing, from the prostration that expresses humble submission to the bold approach to the throne of God with upturned face and raised hands.

Spectator Christianity

I suspect that much of the unreality that so easily creeps into our worship is due to the neglect of this variety of biblically endorsed poses. An action literally puts flesh on to the skeleton of an inward attitude, and fixes it in space and time. Just as the act of putting our thoughts into words clarifies, tests and fixes them, the act of putting our convictions, feelings and spiritual 'stirrings' into physical actions clarifies, tests and fixes them also. It is often far too easy to drift through a service of worship unchallenged and unmoved, simply because nothing demands *acts* of commitment. To act is to test the reality of belief and not to act is often to suspend belief. I wonder how many of us would be forced towards greater honesty towards God and one another in worship and in general, were we to be deprived of the passive 'spectator' roles that encourage us to hold our beliefs in a kind of suspended animation.

It has been proved of course that it is possible to adopt a comprehensive set of devotional actions, a wholesome and rich liturgy of worship, and still to be without the power of God that authenticates true worship. What we need is both the genuine spiritual life within, the teaching of doctrine to enliven and enlighten our minds, and the richness of appropriate modes of bodily expression. Each feeds and stimulates the other, and helps us move towards integrity as human beings. Integrity is a key word here, because God is in the business of making us like Jesus, within whom there was a perfect integrity, not only in the popular sense of the word—that is, truth and honesty—but in the sense of a perfect integration of body, mind and spirit, directed to a simple purpose of pleasing his Father.

Worship and the five senses

If we genuinely believe that salvation is for the whole person, then we must cater for the whole person in worship, allowing the truth about God to be encountered by all our senses as well as by our spirit. The more help we give our senses, the more of the truth about God we may expect to encounter. The very taste and smell of bread and wine can be powerful signs by way of the associations they call up. The waters of baptism are an experience involving all the senses (though this can depend on the amount of water used!) and it could be argued that there is no more powerful a symbol of passing through death and up into life, than one that literally plunges the five senses under gallons of water and then out again! It is a significant and memorable experience not only because of what it speaks of, but because of what it is to our bodies at the time. In everyday life, our eyes are constantly bombarded with images and symbols representing the material paraphernalia of a consumer society, and the seductive art of the advertisers has never been so carefully studied or massively exploited. We would do well to limit where possible what we absorb of all this because it undoubtedly conditions us accordingly, but we cannot go about with our eyes closed! Surely it would go some way to counter-acting the effect of all this if we 'fed' our eyes, and the 'reference library' of our visual imaginations, with images that spoke of Christ.

Much of the artistic heritage of the church originated in the days when only the rich were literate, and the poor were educated by way of picture stories in stained glass windows, symbols and ceremonies. Although now most people can read the stories themselves without the pictures, it is still pictures that have the edge on the other senses in terms of making a lasting impression upon us. As I have already mentioned, many churches have revived the art of banner-making, where themes or Scripture verses are illustrated pictorially on large banners, which are hung in the church at appropriate times according to the current theme of the worship. Such illustrations can preach sermons all by themselves when created skilfully and lovingly under the inspiration of the Holy Spirit. They are a magnet to wandering eyes, and their symbolic content (if portrayed successfully!) can be a powerful stimulus to the worshippers. As further aids to the senses in worship there is the oil of anointing, the laying on of hands, the kiss of peace and so on, all of which help to locate our faith in the context of a material world, and can become a means through which we 'touch' the spiritual world.

Learning to live from the spirit

I believe that it is in those times during which we concentrate ourselves exclusively upon worshipping God, that we can actually learn integrated Christ-like behaviour as a habit of bodily life. We all come to Christ in the first place with a complete set of behaviour patterns, most of which have been built without reference to the living presence of God. This is why for many people conversion is so traumatic, even if at first there is great excitement. The problem is that we are not used to having God inside us! His presence upsets everything, and so it should! We suddenly have a different moral and spiritual frame of reference; we have his voice speaking into unblocked spiritual 'ears'. Our conscience is sensitized and instructed by Scripture, and we enter a state of violent tension between the old long established regime of sinful habit, and the incoming kingdom. Having lived according to the dictates of the mind, will and bodily instincts, we find ourselves required to live according to the gentle but firm instructions of the Holy Spirit. It is true that it is in the humdrum of everyday life that we must work out our obedience to our new Master, but it is there also that we have the added pressure of a world system that demands conformity, trying to squeeze us back into its mould.

Just as a dancer needs the private disciplines of the rehearsal studio in order to become a natural and spontaneous performer, Christians need the practice room of worship to learn behaviour that flows from the spirit out into bodily action. Regular withdrawals into private and corporate worship, where the personality is given over entirely to practising a sensitive response to the Holy Spirit will, among countless other benefits, help to establish new habits for the whole of life, and send us out into the world as reformers, not conformers.

Breaking old patterns

When I was first filled to overflowing with the Spirit, I
found my mind and body completely unprepared for the
experience. As a fairly reserved and conservative person,
I winced at my own attempts to give even the most primitive physical or even verbal expression to it. I remember
gradually having to break down the old patterns, and I
believe that much of this was done in times of private
devotion when I felt most free to vent all my feelings with
impunity! I would determine to express what was inside
and must have gone through the whole repertoire, dancing,
kneeling, prostrating myself, raising my hands, walking
up and down gesticulating, speaking and singing both
with the mind and the spirit! I'm sure that in this way I
began to establish new patterns derived from a new source,
and partly as a result of this I began to enjoy a new
'spiritual naturalness' in everyday life, even to feel more
'myself'.

Discovering a new identity in God

We live in a society that is obsessed with self-expression,
and that's exactly what it gets—self*ish* expression in all
kinds of destructive ways. Nevertheless it is the legitimate
cry of each human heart to be a unique individual who
enjoys life in a rich, spontaneous way, and surely the
Creator made us that way. Sadly but predictably, his
presence is the missing ingredient in most recipes designed
to help you 'be yourself', and it can be a disappointing
experience without him. The cake never rises! But with
the living God firmly enthroned within us, far from being
reduced to subservient nobodies, we become truly ourselves, and 'filled out' to a complete humanity. Through
the practice of worship, the glorious by-product of losing

ourselves in the wonder of God is that we find ourselves and steadily grow to be the unique characters God always intended us to be.

This by-product must not become the reason why we worship, as there is a danger that over-emphasis of this could tend to reduce worship to the level of a kind of therapy or spiritual health-cure. Worship undoubtedly does us good, and is a health-promoting exercise, particularly in terms of mental health, but if this ever became the reason for doing it then it would no longer be real worship, but more akin to self-idolatry—self having become the central object. Whereas in fact such benefits are just part of the glorious spin-off from a life of obedience to God; this is logical when we remember that in the first place it was *dis*obedience that caused all our ills! We derive the most personal wholeness from worship when we completely forget ourselves in the act of it; and when we forget ourselves we can be sure that God is remembering all our needs—'Seek first his kingdom and his righteousness, and all these things will be given to you as well' (Mt 6:33).

The renewing of the mind

Worship helps us to break out of the thought patterns of a fallen world. In Romans 12:1, after Paul exhorts us to worship God by presenting our bodies to him as a living sacrifice, he goes on to say, 'Do not conform any longer to the pattern of this world, but be transformed by the renewing of your mind. Then you will be able to test and approve what God's will is—his good, pleasing and perfect will.' One simple rule that we can identify concerning the content of our minds is this: what goes in must come out. What we absorb, good, bad or indifferent, is bound to affect our thoughts and behaviour. In Philippians 4:8 Paul says, 'Finally, brothers, whatever is true, whatever is noble, whatever is right, whatever is pure, whatever is lovely, whatever is admirable—if anything is excellent or praiseworthy—think about such things.'

Praise and worship involves concentrating our whole attention upon the Lord: his person, his deeds, his promises, his truth, his purity, his loveliness, his grace and excellence. Worship is not compatible with evil thoughts, and we cannot go very far before seeing our need for cleansing (or freedom from Satan's accusations, whichever the source might be). But having moved into worship, our minds and imaginations will be fed with truth and beauty. (See Chapter 14 for more on this subject.)

Jesus' manifesto of the kingdom

In the little synagogue of Nazareth, before a disbelieving congregation, Jesus took the scroll of the prophet Isaiah, and applied the prophecies in chapter 61 to himself:

> The Spirit of the Sovereign Lord is on me, because the Lord has anointed me to preach good news to the poor. He has sent me to bind up the broken-hearted, to proclaim freedom for the captives and release for the prisoners, to proclaim the year of the Lord's favour and the day of vengeance of our God, to comfort all who mourn, and provide for those who grieve in Zion—to bestow on them a crown of beauty instead of ashes, the oil of gladness instead of mourning, and a garment of praise instead of a spirit of despair. They will be called oaks of righteousness, a planting of the Lord for the display of his splendour (61:1–3).

He then went out and began his ministry of making people whole, planting them in the rich soil of his kingdom as 'oaks of righteousness', strong, secure, fruitful people, able to withstand the strongest storm, not just for their own completeness, but for the 'display of his splendour'.

Shall we dance?

It is impossible to talk about the expression of a unified personality without being drawn inevitably to the subject of dance. It is a big subject, however, and I will not attempt any more than a brief look at it, and leave the rest to the experts, confessing also that my own lack of muscular co-ordination can present a health hazard to unwary bystanders!

Dance as an expression of worship to the Lord is no new thing, as it characterized the religious culture of the Hebrews right from the moment of their spiritual birth as a nation. It was on the far bank of the Red Sea that Miriam led a joyful celebration of God's victory over the Egyptians, whose army had just disappeared beneath the waves. 'Then Miriam the prophetess, Aaron's sister, took a tambourine in her hand, and all the women followed her, with tambourines and dancing' (Ex 15:20). Hundreds of years later it was written in Psalm 149: 'Let Israel be glad in his Maker, let the sons of Zion rejoice in their King! Let them praise his name with dancing, making melody to him with timbrel and lyre' (RSV). We read in 2 Samuel 6:14 that David 'danced before the Lord with all his might'.

A no-go area?

It has, however, at various periods of history, and certainly in evangelical circles in England until comparatively recent times, been regarded as exclusively 'of the world' and a 'no-go area' for Christians. This is probably the result of a whole series of influences. There was the Platonic dualism mentioned earlier, and more recent philosophies that similarly elevated the value of the mind above the body. There was the Puritan distaste for sports and leisure activities, the Protestant work ethic that looked suspiciously upon bodily recreation, and the Victorian dislike for individuality and self-expression with its consequent obsession with 'respectability'. Then of course there is the ever-present association of dance with sensuality and sexual flirtation, such that many find it impossible to conceive of dance without such overtones. The residue of these attitudes in our minds makes it difficult for many of us to think clearly and objectively about the use of dance in worship. Added to that; so many of us feel physically awkward, self-conscious or embarrassed at the prospect of it that we would rather avoid the subject altogether!

It is surely a strange contradiction if a church that derives its whole existence from an incarnation, the 'enfleshing' of the eternal Word, Jesus, goes on to negate, fear and even despise its own human flesh that Jesus came to redeem. There are undoubtedly great dangers lurking within the 'flesh', but these are most likely to leap into gear when our bodies are sitting passively in 'neutral' and are not engaged by the engine of the Spirit in serving God! The old saying 'the devil finds work for idle hands to do' may apply here. A body trained and active in glorifying God will not adapt quite so easily to fleshly sins as one that is inactive.

Evidence of dance in church history

In the written records of the church's history there is evidence that dance has in the past been seen as a legitimate and commendable expression of worship. Jerome, for example, who was known as quite a sober fellow, wrote: 'In the church the joy of the Spirit finds expression in bodily gesture and her children shall say with David as they dance the solemn step: "I will dance and play before the face of the Lord".' The 'solemn step' should not be of course misunderstood as meaning 'gloomy', particularly in the context of the 'joy of the Spirit'. There is no lack of evidence either in the Old Testament, or in church history (though there have also been objections to it!), to support the view that dancing, as a genuine expression of worship, is a worthy Christian activity.

The silence of the New Testament

Some people are naturally concerned when they find no direct mention of it in the New Testament, and read into this 'silence' an implication that it was not part of New Testament worship at all. However, it can be counter-argued that if dancing was *un*acceptable, then a direct instruction *against* it would surely have been necessary. This is reasonable to suppose, because the context in which the first Christians worshipped was Hebrew culture and, we have already seen, this included dancing in worship from its earliest history. We often forget that Christianity grew first *within* Hebrew culture, and as an extension of the religious heritage of the Jews. If we are going to speculate, is it not easier to imagine that there was dancing on the day of Pentecost (when by the way, the disciples were considered by their behaviour to be drunk), than a ban on dancing?

Leaping for joy

A short time later, Peter and John did not complain when the lame man who was healed at the Gate Beautiful proceeded into the temple walking and leaping and praising God. Peter and John seemed to accept this extreme physical expression as a legitimate response to a miracle, and when all the people came running to them, astonished at seeing a previously lame man leaping, they took the opportunity to preach the gospel, and 'many who heard the message believed, and the number of men grew to about five thousand' (Acts 4:4). It would not be unreasonable to argue that such exhilarating experiences of the early Christians must have time and time again spontaneously spilled over into dancing, this being one of the most natural responses available to match the events around them! It could also be argued that a decline in joyful physical expression may reflect a decline in the kind of raw faith with which Peter and John 'pulled the trigger' of that amazing episode, when they encountered the lame man in the first place.

The redemption of dance

Forms of dance have in fact always reflected current prevailing attitudes to other people and the spirit of the age, so it is significant to note how in the last twenty years or so popular dancing such as is practised in discos, parties, clubs and so on, has become an increasingly individualistic activity with everybody 'doing his or her own thing' with a minimum of verbal communication. Such dancing is almost totally self-orientated and tends to reinforce a lifestyle dedicated to personal gratification and regarding other people, particularly the opposite sex, as a means to one's own ends. However, it is easy for Christians to condemn the dances of the world out of hand, and to forget that for many people this individualistic dancing offers them the only experience they know of feeling like a whole person; of expressing their emotions; of 'working off' their tensions and frustrations.

Lucian of Samosata said of dance, 'It brings the souls of men into the right rhythm and shows forth in visible fashions what the inner beauty of the soul has in common with the outer beauty of the body, because it makes manifest the point where the two flow into one another.' If it is true that dancing is a God-given (though frequently misdirected and corrupted) way in which to enjoy being a whole person, of expressing in a liberated form a oneness of spirit, mind and body, then rather than negatively condemning the world's dance forms, we should be attempting to offer our dancing to him in worship. In contrast to the world, surely Christians have vastly more reason to as well as a wholeness to celebrate that dance, does not evaporate when the music stops—unlike much secular dance. Many Christian parents fear the effect that dancing to rock or disco music may have upon their children; I believe that they would have much less to fear if their children were brought up to use their bodies in worship as a natural part of family and church life, because then there would be no vacuum in this area of their lives that the world would rush to fill. I wonder how many young people have been lost to the false glitter of the world simply because there was no room in the church for their exuberance and *joie de vivre*. It should be the Christians who show the world how to enjoy life as we celebrate the genuine wholeness that comes from being made complete in Christ. Should not the redemption of a dancer include the redemption of their dancing?

Interestingly enough, the only direct reference to dancing in the New Testament comes when Jesus tells the parable commonly termed 'the prodigal son'. Many preachers would prefer, however, to call it, 'the parable of the elder brother' because it was his reaction to the prodigal's return that was the 'sting in the tail' and probably the main point of the story: 'Meanwhile, the older son was in the field. When he came near the house, he heard music and dancing.... [He] became angry and refused to go in' (Lk 15:25–28). We must of course be careful not to read more into this than was intended, particularly about dancing, but what is clear is that the older son was jealous of his younger brother's 'salvation', did not approve of the forgiving love of the father, and was envious of the celebrations because they were not for him but for his reprobate brother. Those of us who find it hard to accept the sight and sound of others joyfully dancing in the joy of salvation must examine the real motives behind our objections, and question whether or not we may be acting the part of the 'elder brother' ourselves. Having said that, we must not blindly accept everything that goes under the title of worship, but learn understanding and discernment so that we may help ourselves and one another to do what is pleasing to God, and not merely to conform either to the restrictive *status quo* of the past or the new ecclesiastical fashions of the present.

Note: Because the use of dance in worship is such a specialized area, I would not wish this brief examination to be regarded as any more than a stimulus to thought on the subject. As so little written material is currently available on this subject, I suggest that those who wish to look at dance in worship in more detail write for a book list to: 'The Sharing Company', P.O. Box 2224, Austin, Texas 78767, USA.

10

Creativity in Worship

Some time ago, my wife and I were given an old, but functional, colour television. Our redundant twelve-inch black and white portable was removed and we suddenly discovered the world of colour that we had been missing. For a while it even distracted our attention from the poor quality of much of the programme content! Previously we had been looking at exactly the same images, but our set had only conveyed part of the truth about what was happening in front of the cameras.

In a similar way, our manner of worship often falls short of reporting the truth about the object of our faith. Our worship comes out in black and white (sometimes still life black and white!) while the truth is in full technicolour moving pictures. If we are truly called by God to give expression to his character, to be the flesh and blood manifesto of his personality and attributes, then we must learn how to reflect accurately what we 'see' of him, in the richest possible way.

What is creative worship?

It is true of course that the human and finite will continually fall short in attempts to give true and living pictures of the divine and infinite, and I wonder whether eternity itself will ever bring us to the point where we adequately describe God's qualities. Nevertheless, we were made by him in his image, with the intention that our lives should, as it were, hold up a mirror to him. We will never find any greater purpose for our lives than this, and indeed we are promised that one day, when we see him as he is, we shall look at ourselves and discover that we have been made like him (Jn 3:2). We are meant to be the medium through which divine truth is made visible, so to take the TV illustration a little further, our spirits and minds should be like the camera that 'sees', and our bodies, lives and behaviour should be like the TV receiver that makes it all visible. We need to learn both how to 'see' more clearly, and to display more accurately the glory and majesty of God. Much of our worship, because of its 'monochrome' nature, leaves God unglorified, ourselves uninspired and the non-believer uninformed and unimpressed. If a sincere and honest stranger was invited to an average Christian meeting having been told that the Christian's God made himself known in such gatherings, what kind of impression might he get? Would he feel that he was attending a memorial service for a God who is dead, or a celebration of a rich and abundant life poured out by a God who is alive? Would he see the colourful living life of Christ, or be shown something more akin to an old and fading black and white photograph?

Creative worship happens when a fellowship of believers by faith skilfully employ their gifts to give expression to the words, gifts and power of the Holy Spirit within them.

Lack of creativity veils the truth

Even when a group of Christians are experiencing the adventure of God living in them, the fact sometimes remains strangely hidden in their manner of worship and thus veiled to the outsider. There can be a variety of reasons for this, but I believe that one of them is to do with the neglect of our God-given creativity. Creativity is an attribute of God, evidenced by the fact of our own existence and the infinite beauty and variety we see in the world around us. God is a creative God, and he made us in his image as creative people.

We are all creators

It is a mistake to associate creativity exclusively with artists, sculptors, musicians and such like, and by so doing we deny or devalue a large part of our own humanity as people made in the image of a creative God. We often forget that we are surrounded by the products of creative people: the chairs we sit on, the buildings we live and worship in, the words and music in our songbooks, the computers that send us our telephone bills! We are all creators, but there is endless scope for everybody to be more creative, especially when we realize that our creativity is for the glory of God. In relationships, for example, there exists a seriously neglected area of creativity: the art of love. Love for God, love for our families, for husbands and wives, for friends, strangers and enemies. As one who travels a lot and stays in many homes, I appreciate the creators of good hospitality and, in the many meetings I am involved in, the craftsmen of good organization. There is an art in the loving and wise use of words, in bringing up children, in giving gifts and so on, and we must not restrict our concept of creative people to an elite with outstanding talents in the performing arts.

The salvation of our creativity

However, our laziness, our 'busyness' and our capacity for reducing all kinds of human activity to repetitive and unimaginative habits, tend towards a 'monochrome' existence, and both the world and the church gravitate towards uniformity and the false feeling of safety to be found in it. Through sin, our creativity has often become misdirected, used to glorify man instead of his Creator.

God's purpose in sending Jesus into the world was to redeem the whole of our fallen humanity back to himself, to restore in us the image of himself. We have become like those fairground mirrors that throw back a distorted and grotesque reflection of the person who stands before them. God is in the business of renewing our personalities so that we begin to tell the truth about him once more and redeeming our creativity from selfish corruption back to its original purpose. I have touched on the fact that creativity is not solely to do with the arts, but is an integral part of everybody's life and as such is a very broad subject. Hence for the purposes of this book I will concentrate more on creativity in the context of corporate worship, while wishing to emphasize that as a background to this there is also the need for a creative approach to worship in the course of our day to day, mundane living, particularly our worship of God in the way we love people.

You cannot create in a vacuum

To be creative we need at least a little of that sometimes illusive commodity, inspiration. As a writer of words and music I say this with feeling, remembering the frustrating experience I often have when sitting in front of a blank piece of paper that seems only to reflect the blankness inside my mind! Without something to stir my creative energies it is impossible to get much done of any value. The best creative work usually seems to arise out of the 'melting pot' of experience, drawing upon feelings, emotions and convictions that are formed when our lives are under pressure or undergoing changes. Inspiration, in my experience, does not so much float out of a clear sky as get washed up on the beach in a storm! This is not to say that the source of all inspiration is in hard times, but it often takes an extreme of emotion or conviction to crystallize a particular truth and make it real enough to become the raw material for creativity. Bearing in mind that pressure and continual change are two hallmarks of genuine Christian experience, we should not be left for long without inspiration!

The drama of God with us

To put it another way, it is the drama of our lives that provides the resource for creative activity. The more we are faced with the unexpected, the painful, the extremes of joy and sadness, and the starker issues of life and death, and discover the grace and mercy of God as we learn to depend on him in it all, the more we find to say about his faithfulness. When our lives become predictable or boring, there seems little to say that we have not said before. We are at the centre of the greatest drama in heaven and on earth: the incarnation of the Creator God in Christ Jesus, the drama of 'God with us'. The life, death, resurrection, ascension and glorification of Jesus is surely the most amazing story of all time, and the climax of the adventure is yet to come.

Meanwhile, as individuals and as companies of believers, our personal and local dramas continue to unfold each day as God invades, changes and builds his kingdom among us. And all the time he is drawing each one of us nearer and nearer towards the glorious consummation of his purposes for all creation. This real-life drama makes anything that the theatre has to offer pale into insignificance, though it is a sad fact that while many are only partly aware of the enormity of the events in which we play a part, others prefer to stand in the wings and watch more adventurous souls take the 'risks' of living faith.

What releases creative worship?

Taking for granted the fact that there must be something inside us wanting to get out, there are forces working upon and within us that determine to what degree it is released. What we express from the heart is very personal to us, and in a very real way it is an extension of our character. The fact that something is inspired by the Spirit does not always enable us to detach ourselves emotionally from it, and every preacher I know comes off the platform feeling vulnerable, having both opened his heart and taken on the awesome responsibility of delivering God's word. It should be obvious, then, that the more assurance we have of love and acceptance, in God and in one another, the more secure we will feel and the freer we will be to make our contribution. We also need a situation where space is made for even the more timid member to contribute, a recognition that God speaks through every personality and gift, and a sense of expectation, both corporate and individual, that God will use us.

The best way in which we can help our growth in this area is simply by encouraging and affirming one another where gifts are used or spotted in potential.

Developing our skills

Whatever the level of our abilities compared with other people's, we have a clear responsibility to make the best possible use of what we have. The parable of the talents makes this point clear, as do Paul's words in Colossians 3:23—'Whatever you do, work at it with all your heart, as working for the Lord, not for men.'

There is a popular misconception around that using your creativity as a Christian should be like tuning a radio into a broadcast and instantly receiving a completed product. We sometimes hear people say, for example, 'God gave me this song', and after hearing it one is tempted to think that there was a lot of interference on the spiritual airwaves that day! Though there are undoubtedly occasions when there is a special sense of God's inspiration, and the song or whatever it is seems to take shape almost of itself, the general rule appears to be the old formula of 10% inspiration and 90% perspiration! It is interesting to note for example that Psalm 34 was originally written as an acrostic, something that involves a considerable amount of effort, time and skill to create. God has given us creative abilities, and though he may on occasions choose to bypass them, he loves to receive from us offerings on which have been lavished loving care, time and attention to detail. There is an exhortation in Isaiah 33:3 to play instruments skilfully, and in 1 Chronicles 15:22 we read that 'Kenaniah the head Levite was in charge of the singing...because he was skilful at it.' In the exercise of spiritual gifts, skills are also needed. They are like a carpenter's tools which, when handled skilfully with love, wisdom and discernment, can be used to create something beautiful. When handled carelessly or inexpertly, however, they can hack, damage and destroy.

Some areas for creative development in corporate worship

Within the limits of this book it is not possible to go into great detail, and much has already been written elsewhere on most of these areas. In the brief survey that follows, there is nothing startlingly new, but I hope it will serve as a stimulus and encouragement for those who feel 'stuck in a rut'.

1. Music

Music encompasses singing, composing, arranging and instrumental skills. All these are traditionally given more attention than most other areas, but nevertheless many congregations hold untapped abilities and undeveloped potential. Even when basic talent is absent for creating a choir, singing group or small orchestra, we can do much to improve the quality of our singing! The main reason why the Welsh sing better than the English is that apart from possessing a language with a particularly rich tonal quality, they have a tradition of good singing, and a pride in doing it well, that can make excellent singers out of good ones and even average ones out of terrible ones! Where there are people, there are always some who have musical ability. How sad it is when owing to lack of imagination, fear of change, or motivation, people with music in their hearts, mouths and fingers are kept passively in the pews.

2. Dance

Obviously an area with enormous scope for development, this has been discussed in chapter 9 above.

3. The art of reading Scripture

This may sound strange to some, but it is yet another neglected art in worship. Readings need not be just 'read'. For a start they can be read with greater expression, in an attempt to re-create the atmosphere of the event, or the sense of conviction of the writer. If we really believe it is the inspired word of God, we should read it as such, with authority, conviction and compassion. Secondly, certain passages lend themselves to being dramatized using two or three readers taking character parts, or in 'question and answer' passages with one voice asking the questions and another giving the answers. Thirdly, one voice can lead followed by the whole congregation reading the responses. There are numerous other permutations and, of course, this is nothing new, but frequently in the rush and hurry of preparation, it is easier not to bother with the planning and rehearsal required to bring a passage vividly to life in these and other similar ways.

4. The gentle art of silence

In an age of noise, silence can even be something people are scared of, and it seems that fewer and fewer of us really know how to use it in life, let alone in corporate worship. Many of us feel insecure or embarrassed by silence, possibly because we have not learned to concentrate our minds on anything other than the dominant noise that happens to be in our environment at any given time. We also find it easier to talk to God, and sometimes at him, than to listen to him, being frequently more interested in what we have to say than in what he has to say. To be able to spend time sitting silently, simply enjoying the company of another person, shows a great depth of friendship and understanding, and so it can be with God once we get to know him. We must learn how to be quiet and listen, to prick up the 'ears' of our spirit, and to take a word, phrase or verse of Scripture and meditate upon it in the presence of God. Surely all of us would benefit from a course to learn the gentle art of silence before God. The practice of silent worship would, I suspect, make our noisy worship a lot more meaningful too.

5. *One in the eye is worth two in the ear*

The drabness of many church interiors would not only benefit from a coat of paint and a good colour scheme, but more to the point they would benefit greatly from various kinds of visual aids to worship. For example, many churches make their own banners displaying pictorial lessons, illustrations of divine truths, key words or Bible verses and so on. Apart from the visual stimulation that these can provide, the groups that make them often enjoy the great friendship and mutual support that their shared labour creates. It is a widely held view in educational circles that people are twice as likely to remember what they see as what they hear ('one in the eye is worth two in the ear'). I wonder how effective our communication would be if we took notice of this fact and explored ways of illustrating the subject matter of our worship.

6. *Leading worship*

Leading worship is a creative function (see Chapter 13), an art to be learned; a creative approach to planning programmes and services of worship can bring new vitality and interest to them; even the layout of the chairs (if you have them!) done imaginatively in order to set us in the best possible positions for worship together can make a tremendous difference.

7. *Drama*

Drama can be used to powerful effect in illuminating teaching points, bringing to life biblical scenes, and facing us with the challenge of the gospel to our everyday lives. Movement, dance and mime can all illustrate spiritual truths and be a means of expressing praise and worship to the Lord (see Chapter 9). For many people this provides one of the richest ways they know of showing their love and commitment to their Saviour, and many others have been moved and spiritually challenged by simply watching.

I hope that this list helps to remind us of at least some of the most obvious areas in which there is ample room for greater creativity as we ask ourselves the question: What is God doing in our lives? How can we put into words, songs, music, pictures, movements and dances, structures and patterns, signs and symbols, smells, sounds, touch and even taste, what he means to us? How can we be rich in our expression of worship, as he is rich in mercy towards us?

Testing the product

Creative worship often involves using our own words and ideas to express truths, and we must always be careful to measure and test these against the teachings of Scripture and the witness of the Spirit within. I have once or twice, for example, seen dramatizations of Scripture stories that miss the whole point of the original, and heard song lyrics that, though sung with sincerity, are peppered with doctrinal errors! It is vital we bear in mind that to varying degrees what we produce teaches the listener or viewer. We have a responsibility to test the product first, and to ensure that it does not fall short of the truth it is intended to convey. It is true, of course, that in areas of artistic creativity, our perception is to an enormous degree conditioned by our cultural background and predispositions of taste and character. It is important, therefore, that we learn both to apply the objective tests of Scripture, and the inner witness of the Spirit, particularly when our own dislikes or prejudices are aroused!

11

A Perfect Fit

In recent years, much that had been lost in the art of worship has begun to be restored, and much that had become stale and lifeless has been renewed. It would be naïve, however, to think that we had 'arrived' in terms of our understanding and practice of it—if anything, our understanding has outstripped our practice. A show of hands at any truly 'cosmopolitan' Christian gathering will demonstrate that the majority of Christians belong to churches where they still feel trapped in dead or stale forms of worship, or restricted by tradition, culture or prejudice.

'Praise bingo'

One area into which I believe we should venture a little further is that of learning to give praise and worship that is appropriate, that which fits or matches the occasion or the particular purposes of God at the time. The nature and content of our worship should not be an arbitrary thing. Too often, someone calls out: 'Let's sing number 86!' for no better reason than because it is his or her favourite chorus or hymn. Similarly, the worship leader may make arbitrary choices, though I should add that often apparently arbitrary choices turn out to have been divinely inspired! Choice of hymns and songs, however, is just one of the many areas in which we can so easily meander on without questioning why we follow certain habitual patterns of doing things. Conversely, it is possible to pack all sorts of things in just because they are new or different or because somebody wants to 'do their own thing'. We would do well to continually ask the question: 'Why are we using this particular song/reading/tune/piece of drama?' and so on. The question should not be asked with a critical or destructive attitude, but out of a desire to fit our worship into what God is doing among us, in the way that the two pieces of a carpenter's dovetail joint are made to fit perfectly into one another.

Co-operating with the Spirit

In our human relationships we are well used to fitting our words and actions to the occasion. We are not supposed to weep and wail at weddings (except perhaps the bride's mother!), or laugh and make jokes at funerals. It is not usually considered appropriate to send the funeral procession roaring off down the street covered in ribbons and trailing tin cans, or to drive the newly weds slowly away in a hearse!

With regard to the content and form of our worship, everything should be there—or be left out as the case may be—for a reason. That reason may well be no more than an inspiration in the course of advance planning that one strongly suspects has a divine origin, or an intuitive sense of what to do next during the 'flow' of worship. The reason may, for example, be in the choice of a subject by the leadership under the Spirit's directions, which then requires that the component parts are chosen very carefully around that subject. But it is important that worship should have its roots in much more than casual, thoughtless or arbitrary choices. I have previously argued that worship is a response to the activity and character of God, past, present and future. Because he is continually working in and among us in specific ways at any given time, our worship can be a specific response, as well as celebrating general themes that form a necessary background to the specific.

A perfect fit for the occasion

In Matthew 21 we find the account of Jesus' triumphant entry into Jerusalem, followed by his driving out from the temple of the money changers and pigeon sellers, and the healing of the blind and lame people there. In verses 15 and 16 (RSV) we read:

> But when the chief priests and the scribes saw the wonderful things that he did, and the children crying out in the temple, 'Hosanna to the Son of David!' they were indignant; and they said to him, 'Do you hear what these are saying?' And Jesus said to them, 'Yes; have you never read, "out of the mouths of babes and sucklings thou hast brought perfect praise?"'

The Good News Bible puts it as: 'You have trained children and babies to offer perfect praise.'

What did Jesus mean by 'perfect praise!? Is there such a thing as perfect praise outside of heaven? Couldn't it be argued that those children did not really even know the full implications of what they were chanting, having just copied the adults and joined in the excitement of the occasion as children do, carried along by the emotion of the moment?

Whatever else Jesus meant by perfect praise, the way he reacted to the question suggests that he certainly regarded the children's praise as perfect in the sense of being appropriate, a perfect fit. It was appropriate in a number of ways.

Firstly, there was the content. He was being called the 'Son of David', which Jesus knew was a name for the Messiah and therefore appropriate despite the shocked indignation of the priests and scribes who did not agree.

Secondly, there was the manner in which the children praised him. They were 'crying out'. It was a joyful shout of proclamation that the Messiah was before their very eyes, and doing miracles of healing. Gasps of amazement and shouts of joy and praise are surely appropriate when miracles are done!

Thirdly, we must note that it was *children* who were shouting his praises. It was a cry of welcome to a Saviour with whom ordinary children could identify, a working man in simple clothes with a special love and tenderness for them in his eyes. Children are so often mistreated and exploited, and symbolize the innocent and powerless whom Jesus came to set free, so it was also appropriate that praise should come from those who represented the kind of person for whom the kingdom was intended.

Fourthly, the children were praising him in the temple. We must remind ourselves of the significane of what had just happened in the context of where they were. Jesus had just 'invaded' the temple followed by a crush of common people, along with beggars and children. He had completed an unthinkable act of treason in the eyes of the religious establishment by appearing to take over and threaten their control of the very centre and symbol of their religious and economic power, the temple itself. As Jesus literally overturned the tables of the money changers and sellers of creatures for sacrifice they knew beyond a shadow of doubt that their system of power, position, influence and money-making was at stake. It was a racket and everybody knew it (though I suspect it was vigorously justified), but it was run by the rich and powerful and normally no one dared to challenge the system; but Jesus had just done so! In the jubilation of the crowd there was probably some degree of satisfaction that justice was being upheld at last. Those normally excluded from the inner courts of the temple and all it represented for reasons of class, economic status, health, prejudice and possibly race as well, were being led in by Jesus. The joy and power of his kingdom were taking over. Compared to the indignation and joyless legalism of the representatives of the temple regime, the priests and scribes, the simple praise of the children was a perfect fit for the occasion as far as Jesus was concerned. If we compare this occasion with Isaiah 61, which Jesus read in the synagogue at Nazareth and which has been described as his 'manifesto', we may catch a little more of the significance of it, and therefore the ways in which the children's praise was indeed perfect and even prophetic for that dramatic moment.

Everything for a reason

To look at another example of appropriate worship, we can turn to 2 Chronicles 20:1–30. You will need to read the whole story in order to make full sense of my comments on it. The story of the deliverance of Jehoshaphat and the people of Judah against overwhelming odds includes, as the story progresses, many and various acts of worship. Jehoshaphat responds to the news of impending invasion by calling all the people together to seek the Lord with fasting. There are public prayers proclaiming God's power, remembering his past deeds and his covenant with Abraham including the promise of protection. There is an appeal to God's justice to prevail in the particular situation, and a declaration of trust in him alone. There followed God's response in a prophetic word through Jahaziel, bringing comfort, a promise of victory and a precise strategy. Then Jehoshaphat and the people prostrate themselves humbly before the Lord, while the Levites stood up and praised with a 'very loud voice'. The next morning after a fresh challenge to trust God they appointed singers to lead the army out to meet the enemy, in 'holy array' and with thanksgiving on their lips. As they sang and praised, the Lord confused the enemy so that they destroyed themselves. Finally, after the spoil of battle had been collected, they had a day of thanksgiving and blessing the Lord, followed by a return to Jerusalem for celebrations with 'harps, lyres and trumpets'.

A fitting response

Here we see a rich variety in their worship, from fasting to shouting, from prostration to celebration, and everything they did was for a reason. They fasted and prayed because they knew no better way in which to express the seriousness of their appeal to God. They prostrated themselves because they did not know of a more appropriate way in which to express their wonder and awe at such a merciful and powerful God. The Levites stood up to praise with a very loud voice because moderation in volume at that particular point might have seemed to be almost an insult to a God who had just promised a deliverance without moderation! Each stage of their worship was a fitting response to the progress of the life or death drama in which they found themselves, and they did nothing that was irrelevant or superfluous. The irrelevant and superfluous in worship tends to creep in when the drama of our faith recedes. I am aware of course that because the story is about a literal life or death situation the nature of the worship described here is particularly dramatic, but even so there is no reason why worship in less tense situations should not be tailored to fit as perfectly.

The need for a greater repertoire

There is one aspect of this story, however, that should not be ignored. The nation of Judah had a big advantage over many of us in that they had a background of worship culture to draw appropriate modes of worship from, and may well have intuitively known the right responses as a result. Although the religious practice of the Hebrews went through regular periods of decline, it must be remembered that their whole culture was built around the worship of Yahweh and there were established patterns concerning how to do it. While Christians in the twentieth century have had 2,000 years in which to develop a rich worship culture on top of the Hebrew heritage where our spiritual roots lie, most of us are not aware of more than a few scraps of it. It has for all kinds of reasons tended to be reduced down into a severely limited repertoire and become more akin to the surrounding secular culture than to the kingdom of God. The 'rules' sometimes seem to limit us to sitting, kneeling or standing positions only, stiff upper lip at all times please, no emotion. We're British and in church one should be especially British! We need to have our rich heritage restored to us (and it is far richer than most of us realize), to rediscover and develop a worship culture, containing many and varied patterns that will equip us to respond in a fitting way as God moves in, among and around us. (The need for sensitivity in the choice of appropriate material for worship is developed further in the next chapter.)

Building a rich worship culture from old and new

We could start not only by digging into church history and shaking the dust off the forgotten patterns of the past, but also by making a habit of asking God such questions as: 'What is a fitting way to worship you at this moment? What would please you? What would bring us most deeply into communion with you, Father? Which action might bring us closer together as your children?' and so on. We desperately need this kind of discipline if we are to blow away the cobwebs of habit and overcome the common weakness of resorting to the 'safe' and familiar, for no better reason than laziness, lack of imagination or fear of change. Sadly, much of our worship seems designed to fit what pleases the majority (to keep most of the people happy most of the time), rather than what pleases God. There are of course many different opinions about what pleases God, but he is often the last Person we think of asking!

Just as Jesus listened to the children in the temple crying out 'Hosanna to the Son of David' and considered it to be 'perfect praise', a perfect fit for the occasion, he sits invisibly enthroned among us as we worship him, listening and watching for that same perfect fit, and searching for hearts that are concerned to give him the best and most appropriate response as he patiently builds us into a living temple.

12

Leading Worship I

Leading worship—where are we leading people?

The subject of leading worship is a very large one, made yet larger by the vast number of ideas, opinions and traditions that exist concerning what should or should not be done in corporate worship. According to the *World Christian Encyclopaedia* (Oxford University Press 1982) there are 20,780 Christian denominations in the world, and probably each one has a different slant on how worship should be conducted! In the light of that sobering fact, I am not putting forward a pattern to be copied, but attempting to draw out principles that can be applied in various situations. I am concentrating, however, on the leading of open worship where, rather than keeping strictly and exclusively to a preplanned programme, all the participants are seeking to be led creatively by the Spirit into a flow of events unique to that group of people at that point in time. The first questions we must ask when considering the role of leading worship is a question that we often seem to ignore altogether: *where* are we leading people? Hence I will start by trying to locate our destination.

Within the veil

At the precise moment at which Jesus died on the cross a strange and dramatic event occurred in the temple a short distance away. In the gospel accounts of Matthew, Mark and Luke we are told that at the moment of Jesus' death the curtain of the temple was torn in two from top to bottom. To those of us with a limited knowledge of Judaism this event may seem mysterious or even meaningless, but it was in fact a supernatural event of extraordinary significance. The curtain was for the Jews an impassable barrier into the holy of holies, the place where the presence of God was. It was only passed through once a year when the high priest alone entered to make sacrifices for the nation's sin. The rest of the year, and to the rest of the world, it was as firmly shut off in spiritual terms, as Fort Knox is to burglars in physical terms. So what does this mean? The curtain in fact spoke of the sinless purity of Jesus, the perfect standard of holiness that fallen man could never pass through, the barrier which, despite the annual visits over hundreds of years to make animal sacrifices for sin, still hung there symbolizing the disqualification of every one of us from God's presence.

The holy of holies was situated at the heart of the temple, the design of the whole building being based upon the wilderness tabernacle of Moses' day. Before some of you wonder what all this has to do with leading worship, it is important to understand that the original design was given by God as a type, a shadow, a kind of historical visual aid, to help us understand spiritual truths that would find their completion in Jesus.

For over a thousand years a simple curtain had spoken of the barrier between God and man, and then suddenly it was torn in two. It was not torn by men, because it was torn from top to bottom, not from bottom to top. In an

instant it became no longer a symbol of exclusion, but an
entrance, as the tearing of Jesus' body on the cross and the
shedding of his blood became a way into the very presence
of a holy God. Jesus, the great High Priest, had made
once and for all the sacrifice necessary to open the way. It
is significant that in John 1:14, when we read of Jesus that
'the Word became flesh and dwelt among us', the word
from which 'dwelt' is translated means 'tabernacled'. Jesus
tabernacled among us, and in him all that the wilderness
tabernacle signified finds its fulfilment.

We have a temple made of 'living stones'

The holy of holies was the very centre and focus of worship
for the Jews, the place where God dwelt in holiness and
unapproachable light. In Moses' time they had shaken
with fear at his demonstrations of power and righteous
anger on Mount Sinai, and his presence among them filled
them with awe. But now, amazingly, through faith in
Jesus, we are invited right into that holy place, in awe and
reverence, to do what the Jews would have regarded as
unthinkable, to meet God as 'Father'. The gathering together of Christians is now a place where we enter the
holy of holies to commune with our heavenly Father.
Instead of a tabernacle of animal skins or a temple of
stone, we ourselves are the temple, 'living stones' built
together by love and unity, and in that living temple we
are invited to walk through the ever open curtain of
Christ's broken body into intimate communion with God.
'As you come to him, the living Stone—rejected by men
but chosen by God and precious to him—you also, like
living sons, are being built into a spiritual house to be a
holy priesthood, offering spiritual sacrifices acceptable to
God through Jesus Christ' (1 Pet 2:4–5).

When we look around at our brothers and sisters in a

gathering of the church, we should remember that we are all those 'living stones', and that if we are allowing God to do his construction work among us, we can expect to be led into the holy of holies and into an experience of God's living presence right in the centre of our meeting together. Using the visual aid of the tabernacle as our guide, we can gain a most enlightening perspective on worship. I am not putting this forward as a standard approach to a sequence of events in worship or attempting to interpret fully the rich and extensive symbolism of the tabernacle, but it speaks of so many vital principles that we would definitely be the poorer for ignoring it.

'Enter his gates with thanksgiving and his courts with praise'

Our first step is to bring ourselves, setting our faces in God's direction, stepping for a moment out of the distractions of everyday life in order to give our attention entirely to worship. It is a choice we make, an entrance we deliberately step through. In Psalm 100:4 we read the exhortation: 'Enter his gates with thanksgiving and his courts with praise.' About one-third of the psalms begin with praise or with exhortations to give thanks and praise the Lord. Often, psalms would be used as the people processed to the temple, and frequently there is a sense of loud, joyful celebration, an energetic proclamation of thanks for the goodness and greatness of God. It could be argued that strong thanks and praise is the best way of preparing us to draw close to God, enabling us to break free from the burdens of life, and an overconcern with ourselves. Thanksgiving by its very nature turns our gaze towards the giver, and away from ourselves. It causes us to count our blessings rather than our troubles and, most important of all, it gives credit where credit is due—to the Lord!

Having stirred our spirits, minds and bodies into action in this way we have adopted a giving, rather than a taking attitude, forward motion rather than passivity.

Bringing gifts

A worshipper would not enter the tabernacle empty-handed but would bring an offering for sacrifice. While our offering is first and foremost ourselves, as a 'living sacrifice' (Rom 12:1), we do not come empty-handed, and as a token of the fact that we are continually offered up to God, we bring the sacrifices described in Hebrews 13:15: 'Through Jesus, therefore, let us continually offer to God a sacrifice of praise—the fruit of lips that confess his name. And do not forget to do good and to share with others, for with such sacrifices God is pleased.' A person who belongs completely to God will not cease to thank and praise, do good and share with others—his giving to God will be matched by giving to others.

Reminding ourselves of his goodness

Psalms of thanks and praise usually focus upon particular reasons for praising God, and the deeds he has done, his unchanging character and so on, and this is very practical because our hearts often need to be stirred to an awareness of him, and our minds reminded of the marvellous truths about him before we can even begin to expect a 'face to face' encounter! We cannot expect to be intimate with somebody before we have become aware of the facts about them, and their qualities of character.

Clean hands and a pure heart

In the tabernacle worship there is much that speaks about the need to prepare ourselves for God's presence. The altar of burnt offering where the sacrifice in its entirety went up in smoke to heaven, illustrates the need for total consecration of ourselves to God, as Jesus gave himself totally for us. The brass laver, where priests would wash themselves before offering service to God, speaks of our need for cleansing; we should not blunder into the Holy Place without ensuring that we are 'up to date' in cleansing from sin. Psalm 24:3 and 4 (RSV) say: 'Who shall ascend the hill of the Lord? And who shall stand in his holy place? He who has clean hands and a pure heart.'

One with each other

Behind the curtain of the ante-room to the holy of holies we see the table of shewbread. This foreshadows the Lord's Supper and reminds us that we come as members of one 'loaf', part of the same body, and that the unity which Jesus prayed for in John 17 should be maintained if we are to see God's glory.

Enlightened by the Holy Spirit

The only light in this enclosed space comes from the golden candlestick, signifying the spiritual light which the Holy Spirit sheds on the word of God (which the 'natural' man cannot perceive (1 Cor 2:14)). Our worship needs to be enlightened, informed and beautified by the word of God, which is spiritually discerned and not by the natural light of human understanding.

Intercession

In front of the veil of the holy of holies (now torn in two
and wide open!) is the altar of incense, a symbol of prayer.
It signifies the intercession of the risen ascended Christ
before the throne of God on our behalf, and caught up as
one with his prayers are the prayers of people rising like a
fragrant perfume to the Lord.

Awe and wonder

Now we approach our destination, through the torn veil,
the way opened to us by Christ's broken body on the cross.
After the noise of joyful singing, thanksgiving and praise,
we begin to sense the majesty of God and our activity
quietens down to be replaced by reverence and awe.
Having been 'doing' in the courts of praise, here our 'doing'
turns to 'being', our action turns to stillness. In the holy of
holies we find that we can do little but wonder at, and try to
take in, the picture we see of God's grace. We are faced
with the completed work of Christ on our behalf. First of all
we see the sprinkled blood upon the mercy seat, the sign of
our forgiveness, and the price paid to bring us here. We
must cease now any attempt to make ourselves more
acceptable to God, or to punish ourselves for our sins and
failures: Christ has done it all and we are clothed in his
righteousness. Our praise turns to worship and adoration
as we ponder on his great mercy. Before us is the ark and
its contents that speak of Christ and what we may find in
him. (The ark was made of wood but covered completely
inside and out with gold. Wood signifies humanity, gold
divinity, therefore illustrating Christ's nature.)

Resting in his righteousness

Within were three significant objects. First, there were the
tablets of stone on which were written the Mosaic law,
God's standard of righteousness. In Christ the demands of
the law, impossible for us to keep, are totally satisfied, and
not only that, but when we are in Christ we find the law
written on our hearts (Ezek 36:26 and 27). Once again, we
can only wonder at a completed work on our behalf.

Resting in his provision

Secondly, there was a pot of manna, the food that sustained
the Israelites through forty years of wilderness wandering.
In the New Testament Jesus makes a connection between
himself and the manna, and describes himself in these
words from John 6:48–51:

> I am the bread of life. Your forefathers ate the manna in the
> desert, yet they died. But there is the bread that comes down
> from heaven, which a man may eat and not die. I am the living
> bread that came down from heaven.

In worship we feed upon Jesus, who himself is the
sustenance of our spiritual lives, and in whom is the daily
supply for all our needs. In the wilderness there was
always enough manna to satisfy each person's appetite for
the day, and so in Christ we find that the demands of each
day will never exceed the sustenance that he is able to give
us. Again, God's provision is a complete one.

Jesus' eternal priesthood

The third item inside the ark was Aaron's rod. It was a
simple stick of dead wood cut from a tree, which in an
incident described in Numbers 17 was placed overnight in

the presence of God, and by morning it had simultaneously budded, flowered and borne some fruit. This is understood to be a symbol of the resurrection of Jesus from death to an eternal priesthood: 'You are a priest for ever, in the order of Melchizedek' (Heb 5:6). Also in Hebrews 7:24 we read, 'because Jesus lives for ever, he has a permanent priesthood. Therefore he is able to save completely those who come to God through him, because he always lives to intercede for them.' Whereas in the tabernacle there was no place for the priests to sit down, because their work was never finished, we read of Jesus in Hebrews 10:12: 'But when this priest had offered for all time one sacrifice for sins, he sat down at the right hand of God.' Here again our worship reveals a completed work, and because we are 'in Christ', we partake in the power of his resurrection, his new life and fruitfulness and have ourselves become 'kings and priests' (Rev 5:10), seated with him in heavenly places (Eph 2:6), even though our feet are still firmly on the earth.

A place of communion with God

It may seem strange to apply these last three 'types' to our worship today, but I believe that there is a vital significance here for application in our current understanding of where worship should lead us. Too often our approach to God stops short of entering the 'inner sanctuary', and we hover around aimlessly wondering what to do after we have praised, thanked, prayed, sung and so on. These pictures show us that the place of communion with God is a place of rest. The 'rest' is there because in Jesus God has done everything necessary for our salvation and for the supply and sustenance of our lives. There is nothing we can add, and all our strivings and strugglings can and must cease. Hebrews 4:10 says, 'for anyone who enters God's rest also rests from his own work'.

When we enter into the awesome presence of God, his finished work can take over in our lives, and we can go out again into the world knowing afresh where the power with which he builds his kingdom comes from. Not only that but in his presence we will be *em*powered to serve him, having 'tapped into' the source of all power. In that place, we learn to gaze and to listen, to commune with the God and Father of all mankind, so surely we cannot help but come out somewhat changed!

'With angels and archangels...'

We discover also that this meeting point with God is spiritually a meeting point between heaven and earth; after all, as we have seen, Christ is now seated 'at the right hand of the Father'. The book of Hebrews, which revels so much in the heavenly priesthood of Jesus, describes our position under the new dispensation that the tabernacle foreshadowed. Hebrews 12:22, 23 states:

> But you have come to Mount Zion, to the heavenly Jerusalem, the city of the living God. You have come to thousands upon thousands of angels in joyful assembly, to the church of the first-born, whose names are written in heaven. You have come to God, the judge of all men, to the spirits of righteous men made perfect, to Jesus the mediator of a new covenant, and to the sprinkled blood that speaks of a better word than the blood of Abel.'

Here we see heaven and earth all mixed together, which is why in our worship it can sometimes seem as if we are halfway there! When we worship, we literally join in with the praises of heaven, including all the saints and all the angels, and we 'touch' the things that are eternal and unshakeable. It is only this contact with heaven that can give us a true appreciation of God's plans and purposes for his kingdom here.

I have no desire to create out of the lessons of the tabernacle a 'formula' for worship, a strict sequence of events, or a standard 'checklist' against which to measure what we do, and certainly there is no historical evidence in the early church to suggest that they conducted their worship with a plan of the tabernacle in hand! However, the principles embodied in it are put there by God for our instruction, and should serve to increase our vision of where we are going and how we get there when we are given the responsibility of leading people into the presence of God.

> Therefore, brothers, since we have confidence to enter the Most Holy Place by the blood of Jesus, by a new and living way opened for us through the curtain, that is, his body, and since we have a great priest over the house of God, let us draw near to God with a sincere heart in full assurance of faith, having our hearts sprinkled to cleanse us from a guilty conscience and having our bodies washed with pure water. (Heb 10:19–22).

Having looked briefly at the route we are taking, we go on in the next chapter to look at the equipment and skills that will help us to make the journey.

Note: There are obvious implications here for the way in which we use music at the different stages of worship, and this is developed further in Chapter 13.

13

Leading Worship II

Leading worship—nuts and bolts

It should be clear from what we have learned so far, that the task of leading people into the presence of God is a high honour and a serious responsibility. While it is good that in recent times this role has become more open to the ordinary believer, and times of 'free' worship are common in many fellowships, it must be admitted that the job is often done badly. The desire for freedom in worship has sometimes resulted in a 'free for all', ending up in chaos and disorder. Equally, the concept of being led by the Spirit has sometimes given way to a feeling that unless everything that happens is truly spontaneous, it must be man-made and not God-inspired. The kick-back from the rigid patterns of the past is all too often a suspicion of advance planning, firm leadership and efficient organization. How often, though, is the flow of 'free' worship interrupted and the atmosphere marred by musical incompetence, poor leadership or the absence of adequate planning and practical preparation?

First of all—be a worshipper

Leading worship is indeed a role that should remain open
to anybody called and gifted in that direction, but it
should also be seen as an art to be learned, and the
learning of that art should be approached as a serious
undertaking. However, probably the most important
principle of all does not entail technical experience, but
concerns the heart. To lead others in worship, you must
be a worshipper. There is much truth in the saying that
'you cannot take anyone further than you have been
yourself', and if you do not have a real desire to worship
God, you will not take others very far—in fact, they will
probably overtake you! In the midst of all the practical
considerations of choosing songs, sensing the atmosphere,
playing the right chords and so on, the overriding activity
must be to stir up your own spirit towards God and give
him genuine thanks, love and praise.

Be a servant

A worshipper will also display the attitude that is founda-
tional to both the spiritual and practical aspects of Christian
leadership of any kind, and that is the servant attitude.
We looked at how this attitude should characterize our
worship in Chapter 4, but here we are considering the
leader as a servant. Jesus said 'For even the Son of Man
did not come to be served, but to serve.' He lived and
taught servanthood, and graphically illustrated this rev-
olutionary approach to leadership when he shocked his
disciples by washing their feet, a job reserved for the most
menial of slaves.

Leading people in worship must be with the attitude of
serving them, and not as a way of wielding power, or a
means of self-elevation. A good servant is concerned above

all with pleasing his master, not himself, and will take pains to do his job to the best of his ability. He will make an effort to become skilled in the practical requirements of the job, and to build up the resources necessary so that he is always prepared to fulfil the demands of his master.

Practical considerations

If the worship leader is leading with the voice or with an instrument or both, then a reasonable level of musical proficiency is necessary. It is difficult to set a rigid standard for this, because on the one hand there are many people with limited musical training and ability who seem to lead sensitively, while on the other hand there are some highly trained competent musicians who have a 'blind spot' when attempting to apply their skills to worship!

One minimum standard to set, however, is whether a person can maintain the flow of worship without constant interruptions caused by technical ineptitude. On the instrumental side of things there is a minimum standard below which the playing starts to drag the spirit of worship down, rather than lift it. If the attention of the main body of worshippers is repeatedly drawn away from worship to discord or confusion at the front, then it would probably be better to do without instruments altogether!

Be a good workman

Having mentioned a minimum standard, I do not believe that we should be content to remain there! As well as the biblical exhortations to 'make a joyful noise', there are also encouragements to 'play skilfully' (Ps 33:3)! Many of us will have experienced how the skilful playing of an instrument, under the fingers of someone who cares about giving the best to God, can lead into an atmosphere that is especially conducive to worship. However, it is a fact of life that there are not enough of these people to go round! Nevertheless, with practice and a determination to be a good workman, a musician of average ability can provide all that is necessary, and find that his or her offering is a positive help rather than a hindrance to worship.

Repertoire and common-sense preparation

There is an obvious need for a fairly comprehensive re-source of songs, tunes and arrangements, and it is impor-tant that the worship leader is conversant with the best way in which to begin and end a song. The lack of positive 'intros' and 'outros' cause people to stumble into and out of songs, creating a feeling of uncertainty. It is an obvious point but people frequently forget to check in advance that the key is correct. There are few more disrupting experiences in worship that to be halfway through a song and discover that none but a handful of brave (or foolish!) souls can make it to the top note! There is usually no alternative but to stop completely and start again, by which time it may be difficult to re-create the atmosphere. Mind you, it can also have the effect of 'breaking the ice' by helping us all to laugh at ourselves, but that is no excuse for not checking in advance.

Information 'at a glance'

Another simple but frequently neglected point of prepar-ation is for the worship leader to know the numbers of all the songs likely to be used. Even a few seconds fumbling around looking for the number can be distracting for worshippers. Obviously this is going to happen if someone starts a song spontaneously, but as such songs are usually quite well known, it is possible to be reasonably conversant with where to find them if people do need the words. I am not renowned for having a computer-like memory, so I find it necessary to prepare a list of songs complete with number and key, and position it on a clip-board in front of me. This functions not only as a reminder of the numbers —numbers stating in which book, and which keys—but also as a reminder of the breadth of choice available. As I prepare the list I prayerfully consider the choices, devise a basic plan and then add some more options in case they are needed. To this equipment I add any bits and pieces I need for my guitar playing, plus a lighted digital clock to aid my time-keeping!

Learning your stagecraft

It is important to check your physical positioning and place yourself where you can be easily seen. You also need to be close to any other musicians in order to communicate, and to other leaders if applicable. Where microphones are used, they need to be used with care to avoid the bumps, bangs and howls that mishandling produces; and particularly when a system has been put up especially for the occasion, plenty of time should be allowed to obtain a good sound, and to become familiar with its characteristics (e.g. how close to speak into the microphone).

Despite all the experience that has been gained in recent years concerning the use of public address systems, their misuse is still far too often a source of interruption during larger gatherings for worship, and the importance of using them properly cannot be underestimated. Advance setting-up on a technical level and planning on an organizational level is vital to avoid the all too familiar mistakes outlined below:

1. The OHP (overhead projector) screen is too small and not everybody can see properly.

2. There is no blackout and the words projected by the OHP cannot be seen properly.

3. The OHP acetates are not in order, and finding the right sheet is like looking for a needle in a haystack.

4. It appears the OHP acetates were written out by a dyslexic with a broken arm!

5. You stroll breezily to the microphone and it is not working.

6. There are no songbooks/there are not enough songbooks/I thought you were bringing the songbooks.

7. It's ten o'clock and the caretaker is dropping a subtle hint by flashing the lights. He doesn't know that we usually go on until eleven-thirty, and besides the preacher hasn't started yet!

8. The piano is wildly out of tune and more suitable for New Year's Eve at the Rose and Crown than anything else.

9. The piano and the organ are not tuned to each other.

10. The pianist and the organist are not tuned to each other!

To this list could be added innumerable instances where lack of organization and preparation can seriously mar a time of worship. At stake is not so much a principle of efficiency or professionalism for its own sake, but a principle of worship. This principle of worship is that we offer the best we have to God, and surely that should include practical organization of resources and equipment.

Clear communication

If a crowd of people are to be led in the same direction, then it is obvious that there must be no confusion as to what they are being asked to do. The worship leader needs to be able to communicate well, to speak with a clear voice, and to express himself with an economy of words. There must be no ambiguity or uncertainty, and great care must be taken to say things in such a way as to draw everybody into the experience of worship rather than to alienate, offend, or set up tensions between people.

The para-message

Whenever a person speaks in public, there runs alongside the spoken words what is sometimes termed the 'para-message'. This term describes all forms of communication parallel to the voice, such as 'body language', dress, appearance, mannerisms and attitudes. All of us are just as sensitive—if not more so—to the para-message as we are to the words being spoken, and although we are to some extent stuck with our para-message, in so far as it is an extension of our personalities, we must discipline ourselves to avoid behaviour that might distract or irritate. I have sometimes been told by friends that on occasions I distract people by fiddling with the microphone stand while I'm talking. Often I have been unaware of doing it, but the people were not! Such things are usually the result of nervousness and as such can communicate tension to the people and need to be controlled so as not to divert attention.

Eye contact

It is important when speaking or singing to people to maintain 'eye contact'. There is no better way to ensure attention than to look straight at people, moving your gaze around the audience and engaging them briefly in direct eye to eye contact. People then feel that you are talking to *them* and are interested in each one, and not just talking at the ceiling or the floor. It is also a great help in assessing where people are 'at' and being sensitive to them as a collection of individuals rather than as a faceless crowd.

Teaching points

The role of leading worship often includes the need to encourage, inform and teach people about worship, and this too needs to be done well. It is a good idea deliberately to develop quick, precise and sensitive ways of saying what you want to say, possibly with humour and the occasional illustration. The requirement is to use as few words as possible so that the 'flow' is not broken, and to help people relax, feel secure, and understand what is going on.

Don't pressurize

The worship leader must if possible draw everybody who is willing and able into the experience of worship and avoid 'pressure tactics' or 'partisan' attitudes that might lead people to withdraw into themselves or into divisions. People must be set free to worship or not to worship in the way you suggest and any sense of a pressure to conform must be avoided. Instead, people should be encouraged to accept and tolerate each other's differences and to turn their attention away from what everybody else is doing, and what everybody else might think about what they themselves are doing, and on to the Lord. Remember also that you can only draw out of people the potential for worship that is in them at that particular moment and the aim is not to push and pressurize, but to encourage and draw out.

Freedom from chaos

As I have already implied, advance planning and preparation for times of 'free' worship is not to be neglected, and can in fact create more freedom—at least, freedom from chaos. People's attitudes to this question are on the one hand a fear of rigidity that stifles spontaneity and following the Spirit, and on the other a fear of the proceedings getting out of control, or becoming directionless and mediocre. Both concerns are legitimate, and I believe that a balance can be found that satisfies both.

Very simply, there should be advance planning based on prayerful listening to the Lord, intelligent discussion between those in charge of the meeting, coupled with an attitude of flexibility. All those leading or taking part should know the aim of the meeting, the 'ingredients' of it, and any particular sense of direction that has been impressed upon one or other of them in their 'listening'. This may result in a precise programme being planned, but there should always be the recognition that God is sovereign and can choose to overrule even divinely inspired plans. When it comes to the actual celebration, house group or service, we must 'expect the unexpected' and be free to alter or abandon the plans we have made.

Vision

Leading worship is leading *people*, and cannot be detached from the responsibility of standing before God on their behalf seeking their health and welfare. A good shepherd will lead his flock to water and pasture, and so must find out where water and pasture are. This is a shared responsibility and the degree to which it falls upon the worship leader depends on local circumstances, but there will always be some degree of it. While the sheep are feeding, the shepherd is thinking of where to take them next, what their needs are and how those needs can be met, and even in a short time of worship the leader must be moving towards a God-inspired destination, even if he himself may see only one step ahead at a time.

It is a process of active faith to lead people by following the Spirit, but it is not 'blind faith' in the sense that the eyes of our understanding, knowledge, experience and intelligence should be open wide and assessing what is happening. If there is vision, then there will be a sense of motion and direction, and a reason to steer things one way or another. Leading worship is like sailing a ship, in the sense of setting the sails to the prevailing 'wind of the Spirit' and steering a definite course, in faith.

Expectation

If the worship is travelling somewhere, then there will be a sense of expectation, though it may not be clear exactly what is expected, just as a party of sightseers will be excited as they approach their destination yet not knowing what they will see there. In worship, expectation is on three levels. Firstly, there is the level of expectation among the people that will obviously be dependent upon many factors. Secondly, there is the level of expectation of the leaders, hopefully yet higher. Thirdly, there is God's expectation —or possibly the word 'intention' would be more appropriate. The aim of course is to rise up to the level of God's intentions for that occasion. This 'rising up' is vital or else we will get trapped in our own moods, feelings and habitual patterns of behaviour.

Talk to God before you talk to the people

For the worship leaders, the best opportunities for the raising of expectation are in advance of the meeting, when during a time of praise and prayer they can focus upon the Lord and seek to perceive his plan about what he intends to do. The leaders will then go before the people able to stimulate their faith and raise their level of expectation.

This is not, however, the exclusive prerogative of the leaders, as it may be that any one member of the congregation, having spent a similar time adjusting himself or herself to God's perspective, will be able to create a similar effect. In fact, it should be expected that if the Lord has something particular in mind, he may have 'tipped off' one or two people outside of the central leadership group!

Expect the unexpected!

However, it must again be emphasized that whatever may have been anticipated in advance, the meeting itself may not in the end fit exactly with what was expected, and we must always allow God his right to break out of our plans and to fulfil the expectations he has given us in quite a different way than we expected!

Discernment

It is important for many reasons to be spiritually prepared on a personal level in advance of leading worship, not the least of these reasons being the need for discernment. Once again this should be a shared responsibility and not just fall upon one person. Discernment is the ability to perceive clearly what is going on, and in Christian worship this is on both a spiritual and a natural level. It is not appropriate here to go into great detail about the gift of discernment of spirits, and precisely what it is, but there is certainly a need to discern between the good, bad and indifferent contributions that people bring, and the source of their 'inspiration'. Such discernment is important so that the meeting can be kept from wandering aimlessly, focusing on unhelpful things or being dominated by certain personalities moving against the 'flow' of the Spirit.

Weighing what is said and done

In 1 Corinthians 14:29, Paul makes it clear that when contributions in the form of prophecies are given, others should weigh carefully what is said. This, I believe, is simply a way of taking into account our weak humanity, because even when inspired by the Spirit, nervousness, excess zeal, personal bias, inability to express oneself clearly, insensitivity to others or just bad timing, can confuse, add to, take away from or misapply a word from the Lord. There are also rare occasions when someone who is spiritually disturbed, even demonically affected, slips into an open meeting and takes the opportunity to wreak havoc! However, we are far more likely to need discernment between that which originated in a pure form from the Lord, and that which was added by the mind, or emotions, or said at the wrong time and so on.

It is reasonable to argue that Paul's principle of weighing carefully what is said need not be applied solely to prophecy, and that the role of leadership involves maintaining a discerning approach constantly. On the spiritual level we need to develop a sensitivity as to when something 'jars' against the Spirit within us and disturbs our peace, and on the mental level we need to weigh what we hear against the standard of Scripture. There is, however, no short cut to obtaining discernment in worship leading, as it comes through experience and the practice of spiritual sensitivity over a period of time.

Steering without tears (the imperfect leading the imperfect)

Skill is indeed required when there is imminent danger of a meeting being side-tracked or damaged by unhelpful contributions, not least because any number of needs have to be met within a short space of time. Some of the skills needed are listed below:

1. Loving sensitivity

Sensitivity must be shown to the person who makes a faulty contribution in sincerity and good faith. It may have taken courage for them to speak up at all, so do not 'put them down' so that they never open their mouths again in public! It is sometimes wise to treat such a contribution as one of a number of alternatives, saying something like, 'We seem to be moving towards intercession here, and it is tremendously important that we pray for Mr. Smith's gout, but I feel that at this moment we should be taking note of the earlier exhortation to give the Lord a rich offering of thanks and praise so let's sing...' In other words, we are being positive and saying in effect 'that is good/may be true/something we need be mindful of, but something else is better/more timely/more appropriate to the occasion'. Hence, the person will not feel rejected out of hand.

2. Loving correction

Firmness must be shown to the person who makes a contribution out of ill-will, excess emotionalism, unhealthy influences and so on, but sensitivity and understanding must still be applied. The rest of the congregation must know that they are in a situation where there is order and control within which they can feel secure, and where people will not be allowed to get away with causing confusion and error. Furthermore, they need to see that there is love for those who make mistakes or fall into error, as nobody (especially the leaders!) is immune from that possibility. A 'second opinion' is vital in such cases, and a quick consultation with another leader (whether verbally or in sign language!) creates a safeguard and sense of security for both leaders and led. If there is no necessity for an immediate confrontation with the person concerned, then it should be avoided (the person can always be invited to speak to the leader afterwards) for the sake of minimizing the interruption.

If, however, a dangerous or hurtful thing has been said, then it should be refuted and corrected immediately or else the meeting may never recover. If such things are ignored people will find it hard to leave them behind, and the conflict created by it will, if unresolved, dominate everyone's thoughts for the rest of the meeting and beyond.

3. Keeping 'on track'

More often than not, the primary skill required in applying discernment to leading worship is far less dramatic, being simply that of redirection. A lot of the time this may not even be detected by the congregation, and it is part of the job of leading worship to carry the responsibility for the direction, thereby removing any burden from the main body of worshippers. For example, the leader may choose a song, pray a prayer, or introduce an item that by its nature brings the right theme back into focus, without making any kind of verbal comment or value-judgement.

Leading by following

There is a further area where discernment needs to be applied if the worship is truly going to be a corporate expression. It should be obvious that the leaders, though in positions of authority and hopefully under a special empowering of the Spirit, will not have a monopoly on being led by the Spirit. In fact there is a strong sense in which the leaders should be led through the people. The context of Paul's instruction for order in church gatherings in 1 Corinthians 14 is clearly one in which there is no lack of participation from the people. The problem there was not how to stir them up, but how to keep their enthusiasm and sheer volume of contributions under control!

While in current practice worship leading seems most

often to be a matter of stirring people out of inactivity, I suspect that it is meant to be a role of steering and over-seeing the richness of expression that emerges as every-body contributes. The idea of one or two people having an exclusive 'hot-line' to heaven and the rest being in a kind of spiritual neutral zone is, I believe, quite a dangerous one. We should expect God to speak through anyone, even a child—perhaps *especially* through a child because children are not so likely to have 'an axe to grind'.

Hence, the leaders should be watching, listening and trying to discern the 'mind of the Spirit' in people's prayers, choice of songs and so on. As they do so, they will test what is emerging against their own minds and spirits, and act to strengthen, highlight and confirm what seems to be most clearly inspired. This is a very practical way in which to be a servant of the church as the church responds to the Spirit, rather than taking the world's idea of leadership and imposing one's own will on others. Hence, the aim is to lead by following: following the direction in which the wind of the Spirit is blowing among the people, and seeking to draw everybody together in that one direction. To use the analogy of a sailing ship with many sails, such as the old ocean-going schooners, the people are like the sails, set to catch the power of the wind and make forward motion possible, while the leaders are the navigator and steersmen who plot the course and direct that forward motion to take the whole ship's company to the destination planned by the captain.

Musical sensitivity

It is vital that there is sensitivity on the part of the music-ians, and most particularly those leading them, so that what the music 'says' does not contradict what our worship is saying to God, or what God is saying to us. In the early stages of worship, the music has great value as a 'stirring' influence, moving our hearts, minds, voices and bodies into action, turning our attention outwards towards God and one another. A mood of celebration can be encouraged, and fun, laughter, noise and rhythm are not inappropriate as we allow our feelings about God's goodness and grace to overflow. Songs can be addressed to one another as well as to the Lord, providing a source of encouragement and help us to 'tune in' to being part of the body. At this stage, quiet slow reflective music will probably send half the people off to sleep!

Later on, there is a crucial point at which we sense that we are being moved from thanksgiving and praise into worship. The music needs to become less dominant and to lead us into a sense of intimacy, love and adoration. Our focus has now moved on from things about God to the person of God himself, and our attitude changes to one of bowing down in his presence. Sensitive use of music can be particularly conducive to our meditation. Alternatively, the music could be stopped altogether, and just our voices joined in an appropriate song, or it may be that the praise has climaxed in loud applause to the Lord and then suddenly we find ourselves in silence. The silence may give way to the beauty of singing in tongues, or vice versa, but the overriding sense is now of being in the presence of a God who speaks to his people. There may be a word given of prophecy, knowledge, tongue and interpretation and so on that could be responded to in a number of ways, for example, a song, or time of prayer, a reading or teaching from the Scriptures. The result of this time of listening in the presence of God should be that we are spiritually fed, and enter into spiritual rest. It should be obvious that insensitive playing of instruments or inappropriate choice of songs can hinder our entering fully into each stage, and skill is needed both in the actual playing and the directing of the flow from one stage to the next.

Authority

Implicit in what I have said so far is the need for authority and this is derived from some of the following things—the kind of authority Jesus recognized was that which is derived from being *under* authority (Mt 8:9), and being submitted to one another (Eph 5:21). Jesus was under the authority of his Father. Spiritual authority is not primarily derived from title or position but as a natural outcome of a relationship, and if people sense that you are close to the Lord, open to others, and able to lead, then they will follow without great difficulty. Your own relationship with the Lord and the people provides the only valid foundation on which to stand when leading others. Out of this relationship will flow the living faith and steady trust that make the exercise of authority a liberating rather than an enslaving power.

Understanding the context

It is important to understand the nature of different kinds of Christian gatherings—for example, the Eucharist, a baptism or even a funeral. There is a lot of difference between the nature of worship in a house-group meeting and a city-wide celebration, or a prayer meeting and an evangelistic crusade. Careful thinking through of what is really appropriate in each situation is vital.

Humility

Your aim is to become a signpost to the presence of God, not a hoarding advertising your own personality or talents. A signpost needs to be in a prominent position and clearly seen, but its aim is to point away from itself. People should leave a meeting like they end a journey—engrossed by what they have seen on the way and found at their destination, not talking about the merits and attributes of the traffic signs. With all our gifts and talents we are no more the centre of attraction than the donkey that carried Jesus into Jerusalem to the adulation of the crowds. The donkey was very privileged indeed, but just there to serve!

'Ground rules'

I have already presented the role of leading worship as a shared responsibility, even though it may sometimes appear from the front that only one person is doing the steering. This continues the principle of the 'servant attitude', and the way in which right relationships are inseparable from true worship. First of all there is what might be termed the 'moral' requirement for this, which I hope is clear in earlier chapters, hence it is foolish to think that somebody can lead others into the presence of God while neglecting to put right quarrels or disagreements with either leaders or those being led. Secondly, there are some very practical reasons why a worship leader should be in real, open and trusting relationships—some of which should also be evident from the things I have already said. It helps a great deal for there to be a set of 'ground rules', understood generally by everybody and in detail by the leaders. For example, there are the questions of who acts in the event of a crisis; who deals with the 'weighing' of prophecies; can anybody stand up and speak or do they need to ask first; can other elders etc. come freely to the fore and take over; who has the final word on such matters and so on. I remember occasions when I have been leading and something has happened unexpectedly that was beyond my 'jurisdiction' or ability to cope with. It has been a great relief to myself and indeed everyone when another leader has stepped forward and dealt competently with such a situation, and it is a source of security to be regularly working within such relationships where the 'ground rules' are understood.

A caring relationship

It must always be remembered that leading people is an expression of a certain kind of relationship with them and whereas a leader may be looking out on to the sea of faces, each face is relating back to the leader almost as if it was a one-to-one encounter. Therefore the quality of relationship, and the degree of genuine caring that the leader displays, is crucial to the kind of response he gets back. That caring is also measured by the degree of care taken 'behind the scenes', developing among the leadership a quality of friendship and functional interaction that frees the people from worry, fear, uncertainty and unhelpful interruption as they worship.

Be yourself

Probably the thing most likely to inspire confidence is to be yourself. There needs to be a balance here between being natural and unaffected and being aware of behaviour patterns that are a hindrance to others. But people will forgive a tremendous amount if they sense that you are being real and not putting on a front. Naturalness comes when you feel reasonably secure and confident, and are obviously 'at home' with God, and with his people when worshipping together. It can give people comfort when you make mistakes as it helps them to realize that you are human too. It is important to be able to laugh, particularly at your own blunders, and to avoid wearing a spiritual 'mask' or putting on a special voice. Worship must not be treated as a separate compartment from your everyday self, but as an extension of it.

Of course, being yourself does not mean offloading your personal insecurities in public, and it is wiser to share your anxieties and uncertainties only with your co-leaders, rather than risk drawing too much attention to yourself by spilling out your lack of confidence or fear of failure.

If I was asked to sum up the art of leading worship in one simple sentence, I think I would say: be a worshipper, be a servant and be yourself.

14

Transformation Through Adoration

'It's time you changed!' bellowed the preacher. He was quite right. An incriminating list of failures, sins and shortcomings relating to the church had been presented. We were in the dock and the verdict of 'guilty' was hanging over our bowed heads. Once again we confessed our sins and determined that this time we really would try harder. Things would change, they really would. But they didn't. Well, they did for a while, but it did not take long for the ticking-off to wear off, and soon everything was back to normal. Or should I say back to *abnormal*, because at least we knew that our spiritual lives were not what God must regard as normal. How could we change? Surely there was more to becoming Christ-like than making New Year resolutions all the year round! We were stuck in a syndrome that went something like this: 'I've failed—I feel guilty about failing—I must try harder—having tried harder I feel much better—oh dear, failed again—I feel guilty—must try harder'. (Repeat endlessly until fed up or exhausted!) The induction of guilt as a motivation to holiness is not a scriptural principle, but it sometimes tends to be used as if it was! But there is good news for guilt-ridden Christians. The Bible shows us a much better and infinitely more successful way by which to be changed.

To worship is to be changed

It could be summed up in the statement: to worship is to be changed. In 2 Corinthians 3:18 (NASB) Paul says: 'But we all, with unveiled face beholding as in a mirror the glory of the Lord, are being transformed into the same image from glory to glory.' The idea of being transformed by looking might on the face of it seem rather a passive way to go about something that surely requires a lot of effort. But we *can* be transformed by looking. It is not only a fact of spiritual life, it is also a fact of natural life. Even a newborn baby will very soon learn to fix its gaze on the eyes of its mother, who will spend long adoring moments gazing back. Surely this is one of its first messages of love, and without that gaze one wonders how much the child would be robbed of its first and possibly most formative experience of a loving relationship. To use a different illustration, I can remember moments up on a North Wales mountainside, gazing over a vast scenario of lakes and valleys as they subtly changed colour under the setting sun. I don't know how long I sat there but it was getting dark by the time I finally tore myself away. It had a deep effect on me, not only in terms of the pleasure of visual experience and satisfaction, but also by bringing a sense of peace, order and simplicity into my heart. As I walked back down the stony path, I had been changed in some small but significant way.

After repentance—a spiritual vacuum?

Relationships grow as lovers sit looking into one another's faces, and these are often the times when the strongest emotions stir. Who can doubt that this changes people in all sorts of ways! How much more then might we be transformed by gazing with adoration and worship into the face of God? If we are changed by getting to know *people*, how much more profound must be the changes brought about by getting to know *God?* By focusing on this means of change, I am not in any way suggesting it as an alternative to repentance, but it is often true that having repented, we leave ourselves in a spiritual vacuum, having little idea how to introduce new patterns of behaviour where the old ones used to be.

I recently came across a marvellous quotation by William Temple in which he said: 'To worship is to quicken the conscience by the holiness of God, to feed the mind with the truth of God, to purge the imagination by the beauty of God, to open the heart to the love of God, to devote the will to the purpose of God.' If all five of these happen through worship, then what they add up to is not a superficial or fleeting change, but a most radical alteration of our behaviour, even of our personality. Inward changes cannot be regarded as authentic until they have been worked out in everyday life, but I would argue that they are very likely to be initiated in the times that we set aside exclusively for looking and gazing: namely, times of worship.

Transformed into the same image

For me, these thoughts add a new dimension to what might appear to be an unattainable command of God which we read in Leviticus 19:2 (RSV): 'You shall be holy; for I the Lord your God am holy.' If we put this verse alongside the one in 2 Corinthians 3:18 that we have just looked at, then we may see a practical way to be holy. By meditating upon God's character, by praising, adoring and worshipping his qualities in detail, by allowing the eyes of our spirit to gaze into his, we will begin to discover our own behaviour altering to reflect what we have seen.

Having looked at the passage in 2 Corinthians 3:18, we

must be careful not to miss the fact that Paul talks of this gaze upon the face of the Lord in the plural: 'But we all, with unveiled face...' Without wishing to duplicate the subject matter elsewhere in this book on corporate worship, it is important here to appreciate that God chooses to reveal himself in a special way when we worship together. As each of us comes with a contribution (1 Cor 14:26), it is as if God gives everyone a small piece of a jigsaw puzzle. As we each add our piece, at the right time and in the right place, the picture God wants to show us begins to take shape, and without doubt it will show us more of himself. Were we to stay at home with our little piece of jigsaw, we may catch only a small glimpse of the Lord's glory and therefore have much less of his glory to reflect.

Mirrors and diamonds

There is also the very real sense in which the glory of God is revealed, not as a vision floating somewhere in the middle distance of our spiritual perception, but actually in the faces of the people with whom we are worshipping. We know that we cannot see the physical face of Jesus, but if, as the passage says, we are all reflecting the glory of his face, then why don't we look in the mirrors all around us? As we enter together into the glory of God's presence, we become surrounded by as many unique reflections of him as there are people in the room! Our mirrors may be flawed in places but his reflection is there if we look carefully. We are all so different, and we sometimes find that we will all reflect a unique aspect of the Lord's character and of the truth he wants to reveal to us.

Alternatively, we could see ourselves as a single diamond with many facets. To appreciate fully the beauty of a diamond, you need to turn it in your fingers and study the variety of reflections within those many facets. The beauty of a diamond is in the interaction of light between the facets, just like so much of the beauty and transforming power of our worship is in the interaction between us, as we reflect the spiritual light of God in our lives.

An uninterrupted gaze of the spirit upon God

This powerful principle needs to be allowed to operate as we set aside times for corporate worship, but it need not be thought of as applicable only to such times. Surely its effect is going to have a much greater transforming influence if it is possible to practise adoration as a habit of everyday life. There are many encouragements in Scripture towards this end, but I will simply attempt to highlight one or two of them. Again, our supreme example is Jesus, who practised an uninterrupted spiritual gaze upon his Father: Jesus gave them this answer: 'I tell you the truth, the Son can do nothing by himself; he can only do what he sees his Father doing, because whatever the Father does the Son also does. For the Father loves the Son and shows him all he does'. (Jn 5:19, 20). Jesus' spiritual eyes never looked away from the loving gaze of his Father. There was only one moment when this happened, one of utter devastation when on the cross Jesus looked and saw only blackness. He cried out in agony: 'My God, my God, why have you forsaken me?' It is significant that this is the only prayer recorded when Jesus did not call God 'Father'.

He was spiritually 'focused' such that at every moment he could 'see' his Father's intentions, and act accordingly. How we love to make our own way through our everyday lives, taking pride in our wisdom and understanding as Christians yet often without even a glance at our Father's face. A child learns to read its father's face remarkably well and will look into it for approval, for a 'yes' or a 'no', and a hundred other silent but clear messages. This is in spiritual terms what Jesus practised—is it not good enough for us? Do we know what our heavenly Father feels about a situation in which we happen to find ourselves? Do we find ourselves having been prepared in advance when we un-expectedly need wisdom and insight, simply because in the course of our habitual looking at God, he gave us that wisdom and insight even before we knew it was going to be necessary? Jesus never applied formulas, even scriptural ones, to the encounters he had with people. Each conver-sation was different; for example, he didn't tell Nicodemus about 'living water', or the Samaritan woman about being 'born again'; Zacchaeus wasn't told about not giving the children's bread to the dogs, nor did he invite himself to the Syro-Phoenician woman's house for a meal! In each situation his uninterrupted gaze saw his Father doing something unique and special. How could we not be radically changed, even transformed, in our mundane lives and indeed see transformations in the lives of those we meet, were we to follow Jesus' example in this way.

'I have set the Lord always before me'

In Psalm 16:7, 8, David writes: 'I will praise the Lord, who counsels me; even at night my heart instructs me. I have set the Lord always before me.' The passage from which this comes is quoted by Peter on the day of Pentecost as referring prophetically to Jesus, so obviously David in his own devotions got 'carried away' in the Spirit and found himself writing prophetically of the Messiah. It is reason-able however to surmise that David himself was able to say: 'I have set the Lord always before me' and we can gather from his psalms that he spent much time in medita-tive worship of the Lord. (The Bible does not, however, gloss over David's lapses of obedience to God.) One could even argue that this habit was the key to his greatness. It was certainly the key to his intimate relationship with God. But how do we actually practise this amid the hectic business of living? Isn't it unreasonable to expect us to do anything more than snatch a moment here or there for a quick prayer, probably an emergency 999 one, at that!

David's words imply a deliberate act of the will, a conscious focusing of his natural and spiritual faculties upon his Maker, the nurturing of a habit over many years, such that even in the unconsciousness of sleep his whole being remained in divine communion. The key to entering into this level of communion with God lies, I believe, in the exercise of a discipline of personal praise and worship, and this is dealt with in the next chapter.

15

Personal Discipline in Worship

As long as I live it shall be a rule engraved on my tongue to bring praise like fruit for an offering and my lips as a sacrificial gift. I will make skilful music with lyre and harp to serve God's glory, and the flute of my lips will I raise in praise of his rule of righteousness. Both morning and evening I shall enter into the Covenant of God: and at the end of both I shall recite his commandments, and so long as they continue to exist, these will be my frontier and my journey's end.

Therefore I will bless his name in all I do, before I move hand or foot, whenever I go out or come in, when I sit down and when I rise, even when lying on my couch, I will chant his praise.

My lips shall praise him as I sit at the table which is set for all, and before I lift my head to partake of any nourishment from the delicious fruits of the earth.

When fear and terror come, and there is only anguish and distress I will still bless and thank him for his wondrous deeds, and meditate upon his power, and lean upon his mercies all day long. For I know that in his hand is justice for all that live, and all his works are true. So when trouble comes, or salvation, I praise him just the same (Column X, 'Manual of Discipline', *Dead Sea Scrolls*).

Personal discipline in private worship

The popularity of the word 'discipline' is probably at an all-time low, calling up images of headmasters with canes, detention after school, and government establishments designed to deliver short, sharp shocks. But if we can manage to put aside for a moment emotive images of cold showers and forced runs around the football pitch, and consider what discipline for a Christian might in fact mean, we could be on the edge of a discovery that can transform our lives.

The word 'disciple' has a much warmer feel to it; a disciple is a person under the discipline of his teacher, and we as Christians should be under the loving but firm discipline of Jesus. Bearing in mind the negative connections that the word has for many of us, we must remind ourselves that the discipline of Jesus is the route into perfect liberty, and lack of his discipline is a sure way in which to become imprisoned. It follows that the most liberated worship is most likely to arise among people who practise a discipline of worship, both in their workaday lives, and in their worship together.

The will

It is impossible to separate personal discipline from a constant use of the words 'I will', and it is interesting that time and time again the psalmists of the Old Testament begin their move towards God by saying it. For example, in Psalm 57:7, 'My heart is fixed, O God, my heart is fixed; I *will* sing and give praise' (AV). This psalm is a psalm of David, and his determination to praise takes on a further significance when it turns out that at the moment of writing he was a fugitive of Saul, hiding in caves in fear of his life. His praise was clearly based on far more than circumstances and mood. It seems that there is a popular misconception around concerning worship, that is, that it 'comes over you' and before you move, you have to be moved. While it is true that worship is a response to God, it is also true that we are frequently blind to his qualities and deeds until we determine to open our spiritual eyes and step closer to him in praise and thanksgiving. The most beautiful views are seen only by those who first determine to climb the mountain. This principle is borne out by James 4:8: 'Come near to God and he will come near to you', and though there are marvellous times when we are unexpectedly caught up in a spirit of worship, these may well be too rare to sustain us for long.

But I don't feel like praising...

There is another reason why God has made room for human initiative in coming to him, and that is his desire to receive voluntary worship, worship that we freely choose to give him. It costs far less to be wafted into worship on a passing breeze, than to determine to give it because we reckon that God is worth it, however we feel. We must also be realistic and remember that we will experience times when our circumstances and feelings in themselves give us no reason to praise at all. These are times when our worship will dry up, unless we have learned to say as did Habakkuk, when he saw a terrible vision of approaching calamity, 'yet I will rejoice in the Lord, I will be joyful in God my Saviour'. Sometimes worship starts because it is felt spontaneously in the heart, sometimes it is an act of the will. Either way, God is equally worthy of our worship, and it is his worthiness that is the important thing, not our fickle and unreliable feelings.

Our part—God's part

We must not, however, be mistaken into thinking that the will to worship can by itself produce true worship. As Richard Foster says:

> It is kindled within us only when the Spirit of God touches our human spirit....We can use all the right techniques and methods, we can have the best possible liturgy, but we have not worshipped the Lord until Spirit touches spirit....Until God touches and frees our spirit we cannot enter this realm. Singing, praying and praising all may lead to worship, but worship is more than any of them. Our spirit must be ignited by divine fire. (*Celebration of Discipline,* Hodder & Stoughton, pp. 138–9.)

The will to worship is our part, while God's part is to supply the fire that ignites it within us.

Shaking ourselves into action

So in what areas can we apply the will to worship? If we look at Psalm 103:1 and 2, we see the psalmist applying his will to stir his whole being: 'Praise the Lord, O my soul; all my inmost being, praise his holy name. Praise the Lord, O my soul, and forget not all his benefits.' He is talking to himself, stirring himself into action on every level. He is, as it were, shaking himself by his own lapels, picking himself up out of his slumber or apathy, and demanding obedience of all his faculties. 'Inmost being' must refer to spirit and emotions, and in addition he is deliberately concentrating his mind to 'forget not all his benefits'. In stirring up his inmost being, there will inevitably be bodily expression of praise, so his whole self is brought into play. The discipline of worship requires that we stand in complete readiness for obedience to the Spirit, like a soldier preparing himself for action.

To praise or not to praise

I remember clearly an occasion on which this lesson was firmly printed on my mind. I had been invited to lead worship at a church some hours drive away from my home, so my wife and I set off early that morning in the rather ramshackle Morris 1000 van we had at the time. It was cold and icy, and the wind blew freely through the many gaps and holes in the vehicle! I was in a grumpy mood, and proceeded reluctantly, creating tension between the two of us. At the time I was spiritually dry, and had no desire or motivation to travel such a long way, let alone to lead worship! By the time we arrived, my mood was blacker, the tension tauter, and the temperature colder.

For the duration of the last five minutes prior to facing the crowd of enthusiastic would-be praisers, I knew I faced a stark choice: to get right with the Lord, my wife (and the car!) and go on in raw faith, or be honest with my hosts about my state and back out!

Probably motivated at least in part by pride, I decided on the former course of action, confessed my sin, apologized to my wife and stepped into the meeting saying to the Lord something to the effect of, 'Lord, I'm empty, I don't feel like worshipping you. I have nothing to give to you or with which to lead the people, unless you give it to me. But, sink or swim, here I go!' From the moment I began to lead the praise, my heart filled up and so we praised with freedom and joy. I did not have to pretend, or put on an act, but because I determined to praise the Lord ignited praise within me, and I genuinely overflowed.

An inconvenient lesson to have learned!

At times I would like to forget that lesson, and those times are when I am not leading but instead am part of the congregation, and feeling similarly fed up and grumpy. I would like to use my mood as a legitimate excuse not to join in, but (to the irritation of the less noble side of me!) I now know that my feelings need not rule my spirit.

The discipline of thankfulness

In 1 Thessalonians 5:18 we read: 'Give thanks in all circumstances, for this is the will of God in Christ Jesus for you' (RSV). This surely involves a discipline, if for no other reason than that we do not necessarily feel thankful about everything that happens to us! Before we can start thanking God for the difficult circumstances, however, we must make a habit of thanking him for the good ones. This is such an obvious thing, but many of us take for granted the good things of life, natural and spiritual, forgetting to thank the Giver. It is our preoccupation with 'getting' that robs God of the thanks due to him, and turns so much of our praying to selfish ends, so that we become beggars in the presence of God instead of worshippers.

For this reason Paul tells the Philippians to give thanks alongside their asking: 'Do not be anxious about anything, but in everything, by prayer and petition, *with thanksgiving*, present your requests to God' (Phil 4:6). Have you noticed how that when we say a sincere 'thank you' to somebody, we automatically look them in the face and smile? Not to do so could seem impolite, if not rude, and I suppose that the times when we do not are usually the times when we are not really grateful at all! Thankfulness is a way of turning our faces towards God, and reaffirming our warm relationship of grateful dependence upon him.

In all circumstances?

The three words 'in all circumstances' are sometimes hard to come to terms with. Often we will feel much more like placing a vigorous or bitter complaint about our circumstances before him. This is where a stronger discipline is needed, but determining to give thanks at these times is not based upon mindless conformity to an unreasonable command, neither are we required to be dishonest. We may quite understandably feel 'How can God expect me to thank him for my being made redundant/the news that so and so has cancer/my overdraft/my failure to keep control of the children, etc.'. The truth of the matter is that if our lives are offered up to God, nothing that happens to us can separate us from his love, faithfulness and mercy, or take us beyond his sovereign control over our circumstances. The problem comes when we do not really believe that! In Romans 8:28 we read, 'And we know that in all things God works for the good of those who love him.'

This does not mean that everything that happens to us comes from God, and certainly we are not being asked to thank him for evil, but we can thank him for the fact that *in* all things, *in* all circumstances, he is still working for good. (It is significant that in the story of Job, the devil had to ask permission of God before bringing troubles to him, and all that happened was allowed by the Lord as a test. At no point would the devil go beyond the limits that God set. Let us not forget, however, that the promise in Romans 8:28 is to those who love God.) God is able to overcome evil with good, turn even the bitterest experiences of life into lessons about his grace and create glorious endings to sad stories.

Turning to God in frustrations

A chance meeting with someone I had not seen for about seven or eight years recently brought vividly home to me the way God can use even the most mundane situations if we offer them up to him in a positive and thankful attitude. I first met Max and three of his friends during a mission in Birmingham when they were teenagers at school and I was in a mission team running a coffee bar and visiting schools. They travelled quite a long way one evening to the coffee bar in the centre of Birmingham, and after spending some time there needed to get home by the times stated by their respective sets of parents. Two of us decided to make the necessary detour in the team's van and set off. Being unfamiliar with the area we soon got lost, and the time by which they should have returned passed. Tension increased as the prospect of being greeted by irate parents loomed large in all our imaginations!

Although our passengers were non-Christians, we decided to stop and pray very simply to find the route and concerning the situation with regard to their parents. Max describes this as the first time he had ever heard anyone pray as if God was real, personal and interested in such matters, and it left a powerful impression on him. For us, it was fairly routine. The next day at school the four friends compared their parental reception committees with those of the night before. They were identical; each set of parents remarked on how early they were! This simple experience of God being brought into a minor crisis was the thing that clinched Max's decision to become a Christian, and he himself is now involved in evangelistic work.

It is sobering to speculate on whether or not he would now be a Christian had we succumbed to the temptation to frustration, irritation or worry in that van, and treated the situation as an annoyance to be endured rather than an opportunity for God to step in. The discipline we need is to offer up to him with thankfulness whatever comes our way, believing against emotion, sometimes against reason, against the apparent facts, that God is still working for good, and has not abandoned us.

Praise is not a 'lucky charm'

We must, however, beware of the danger of using the

words 'Thank you, Lord' as a kind of lucky charm when things go wrong; it is rather an affirmation of faith and trust in God's promises, the vocalizing of a preparedness to risk everything on God, however faltering or mixed with doubt that trust might be at first.

Stepping through the broken glass

The Bible speaks in many places of a 'sacrifice' of thanksgiving, and this makes it clear that it is sometimes costly. It costs us to abandon our self-pity, our blaming of others, our false comforts and escape routes that we have substituted for a trust in God. Romans 1:21 shows us that the consequence of unthankfulness is that thinking becomes futile and our hearts are darkened, but Colossians 1:12 shows us that giving thanks is a practice of those who share in the 'kingdom of light'. Giving thanks is a step from darkness into light, and the discipline of thankfulness means that we take that step not only when our feet are swift with joy, but also when they are heavy with weariness, doubt and fear, and it seems that the route to God is strewn with broken glass.

The discipline of continual praise

Praise and thanksgiving are closely related and similar principles apply to both, not least that both are to be practised continually. Hebrews 13:15 tells us: 'Through Jesus, therefore, let us continually offer to God a sacrifice of praise', and David writes in Psalm 34:1: 'I will extol the Lord at all times; his praise will always be on my lips.' Most of us, however, practise spasmodic praise, depending upon our feelings and circumstances, alternating between praise and grumbling. To be honest, I am often suspicious of people whose every other phrase seems to be 'praise the Lord' or 'Hallelujah', because sometimes it turns out to be just froth and bubble that blows away when things get tough. Many of us have been put off expressing praise in everyday life because of the suspicion, that it is little more than false piety or conformity to a religious 'type', and indeed it is true that many people put on a 'spiritual' front in order to impress others.

Our resistance to it, however, may sometimes have its roots in our 'self-image'. Our picture of ourselves may not include overt expressions of praise, and we know that we would feel awkward or embarrassed were we to do it. It would be 'out of character'. Sadly it is more socially acceptable to grumble and complain, than to give thanks and praise and, sadder still, many of us are more subject to social convention than the prompting of the Spirit. Here we must be open to the power of God to change us, and not regard our self-image as unchangeable or social convention as unbreakable. At the same time we must seek to be genuine and real in our praise and ready to explain our thankfulness intelligently to mystified non-believers.

Our zeal in praise needs to be tempered by a sensitivity to others and we might do well to consider the wise and realistic words of Proverbs 25:20, 'Like one who takes away a garment on a cold day, or like vinegar poured on soda, is one who sings songs to a heavy heart'! There is also the 'back-slapping' praise enthusiast referred to in Proverbs 27:14, whose *bonhomie* is not necessarily welcome or helpful: 'If a man loudly blesses his neighbour early in the morning, it will be taken as a curse.'

Is continual praise practical?

We still have the question of how we can practise 'continual praise'. It is obvious that for much of the time our minds and bodies are occupied with working, eating, sleeping etc. and our attention absorbed by the legitimate demands of living. One could reasonably conclude that continual praise is just not practical and, not only that, if we constantly punctuated our conversation, telephone calls, business letters, meals and so on with 'Hallelujahs', we might become a nonsense, and an irritation to those around us.

'Praising God with your spirit'

There is, however, a level on which our praise can be continual, and that is on the level of the spirit. Our worship is 'in spirit' (Jn 4:23, 24) as well as on a mental and bodily level. Paul says in 1 Corinthians 14:15, 'I will pray with my spirit, but I will also pray with my mind; I will sing with my spirit, but I will also sing with my mind. If you are praising God with your spirit. . . .' Through the Holy Spirit, our own spirits have been brought to life and function, and now we are able to pray and praise with our spirit.

The marvellous thing about the operation of the spirit is that it can function in parallel with our conscious self but independently of it. A friend of mine relates the following experience: 'The day after I first spoke in tongues I was cycling to work and thinking about some shopping I had to do on the way. After a while I became aware that at the same time as my mind was concentrating on my shopping list, my spirit was concentrating on God, praising him in my new prayer language – something was going on in me on two levels at once. Suddenly I understood a little more about what Paul must have meant by continual praise. Hence I found myself thinking about a shopping list and praising God at the same time! I was so excited at this discovery that I almost fell off my bike!' As well as a conscious, deliberate focusing of our attention on God in the nitty gritty of normal, everyday living, praise is an opening of ourselves to the Spirit so that he can bypass our minds and maintain an uninterrupted communication with the Father.

Keeping the engine 'ticking over'

It is clear that the gift of tongues is primarily for the personal edification of the believer (except when used with the gift of interpretation), and is a very practical way of giving continual praise to God. With practice it is possible to get into the habit of continually praising God on this spiritual level (silently of course in the presence of others!) so that it can be likened to keeping an engine 'ticking over'. It is then a straightforward matter, when an opportunity comes for vocal praise in hymns and songs and so on in the vocabulary of the understanding, just to 'put your foot down' and off you go!

Paul implies that not everybody enjoys the benefit of this marvellous gift, but for all of us our birth-right as members of God's family is a reborn, enlivened and active spirit, which under the inspiration of the Holy Spirit will cry out 'Abba Father', and seek ceaseless communion with him whether our bodies and minds are working or sleeping, relaxing or worshipping.

Praise is a public witness

Praise can be a constant 'internal' activity, but the kind of praise God wants is also vocal and audible, because he wants other people to hear it as well as himself! Praise is a strong public witness to others, an encouragement to believers, and a proclamation to non-believers. Psalm 18:49 states, 'Therefore I will praise you among the nations, O Lord; I will sing praises to your name.' Praise can have an evangelistic effect as described in Psalm 40:3, 'He put a new song in my mouth, a hymn of praise to our God. Many will see and fear and put their trust in the Lord.' And in Psalm 40:9 David makes it clear that the truth about God should not be kept secret:

I proclaim righteousness in the great assembly; I do not seal my lips, as you know, O Lord. I do not hide your righteousness in my heart; I speak of your faithfulness and salvation. I do not conceal your love and your truth from the great assembly.

Praise is a way of proclaiming the reality of God in our lives, of making known his character and his deeds to the world.

Personal discipline in corporate worship

Being there

You look out of the window as the cold dark evening draws in. It is raining. Not only that, but the car is in for repairs and you will have to use the bicycle. That's if you go at all. Last week it was a disappointment, and tonight you're tired. The central heating is on and a warm sleepy feeling is beginning to pervade the corner of the room occupied by the armchair. To go or not to go, that is the question. The meeting starts in twenty minutes and it takes ten minutes to get there. Oh no, the bike! It will take at least twenty. Your sense of duty wins and you rush around looking for the bicycle clips, treading on the dog as you head for the door, and out into that unique sense of dampness and gloom that only an English winter can conjure up. As you hunch yourself against the cold and pedal furiously, your mind is a jumble of thoughts – why didn't you put the car in a day earlier then you wouldn't have to cycle tonight – I hope it's worth going – disappointing last week – I must get round to papering the bathroom – that telephone bill was a bit of a shock – now is it quicker to cut through the Grove, or is the hill steeper that way?— that new head of department looks like a bad-tempered type, I'll tread carefully there.

You arrive, and puff and drip your way into the hall,

late. About half an hour later, you are just beginning to enter a moderately suitable frame of mind for worship. Just then the worship ends and the speaker stands up to speak. Oh no! Not him again! By the end the dampness seems to have pervaded not only your socks but your soul, and you just want to get back home to the warm before anyone inquires too deeply about your inward state!

Disciplines of preparation

So many of us end up slumped in meetings in the frame of mind described (with feeling!) above. Usually, however, it is just not necessary, and even when the rush of our circumstances is beyond our control, we can do a great deal to ensure that we arrive inwardly, if not outwardly, ready to step into God's presence. If there is an area of discipline that can transform corporate worship more than anything else, I believe it is that of preparing ourselves beforehand. The background to any preparation should of course be our efforts to cultivate a lifestyle of thankfulness and praise, so that our gathering for corporate worship becomes an extension of, and a genuine overflowing of, a daily walk with God. If this is not the case, we will often find our entering into God's presence to be a violent wrench from a state of spiritual inertia and from a mind-set that is reluctant to adjust to worshipful activity. Rather than stepping suddenly from the gloom into a bright light, to find our eyes dazzled and out of focus, we should each come with our own light already brightly burning to enjoy the greater brightness that comes as we join our lights together.

'Tuning-in' to God

Richard Foster says:

> The first avenue into worship is to still all humanly initiated activity...we are to live in a perpetual inward listening silence

so that our words and actions have their source in God. If we are accustomed to carrying out the business of our lives in human strength and wisdom, we will do the same in gathered worship. If however, we have cultivated the habit of allowing every conversation, every business transaction, to be divinely prompted, that same sensitivity will flow into public worship. (*Celebration of Discipline*, Hodder & Stoughton, pp.144 and 145.)

With this in mind there are also specific ways in which we can make ourselves ready in the time immediately preceding a gathering of God's people.

What did I get—how did I do?

Let us start with our attitude to corporate worship. As members of the consumer society, it is all too easy to find that our predominant attitude, even to worship, is that of the consumer. Unthinkingly we come along to view the goods on display and take what we fancy. We come away complaining, 'Well, I did not get much out of that', and over lunch or supper we evaluate the 'performance' of the pastor or leaders; 'roast preacher' is a staple Sunday diet all over the world. We are concerned with whether or not it was to our personal taste, or emphasis, and how much it met our needs. Those of us who lead often become preoccupied with how well we did or did not do, whom we pleased or displeased. We cannot of course ignore entirely these attitudes in so far as they spring out of what and who we are, but all too often we allow such selfish attitudes to dominate our experience of worship, and we let them reign unchallenged.

I'm here for God and you

First of all, it is not for our own benefit that we come, but for the benefit of our God, to honour, praise and thank him, to give him joy and pleasure in the company of his redeemed people, his beloved children. We should come asking the question, 'Lord, what will give *you* pleasure in our worship, how can I serve *you* and honour *you*?' From this springs the second reason for coming together, that we are there to build up one another. We should come asking the question, 'Lord, how can I serve my brothers and sisters here, is there an individual who needs my friendship or special encouragement or a gift of some kind?' If we come *to give,* to God and each other, we will enter a whole new experience that our selfishness would otherwise disqualify us from.

So what about ourselves? We surely should not ignore our own needs and pretend they are not there? The principle that operates here is the one presented to us by Jesus himself in Luke 6:38 (NASB): 'Give, and it will be given to you; good measure, pressed down, shaken together, running over, they will pour into your lap. For whatever measure you deal out to others, it will be dealt to you in return.' If we concern ourselves with pleasing God, and seeing to one another's needs, God clearly promises that he will look after our own needs. Give, and it will be given to you. How many of us become dry and empty in our worship, even bored with it, and never consider that it may be because we are coming as consumers rather than givers?

Limbering up

Having established our attitude as one of giving, what can we do practically to prepare ourselves? The mime artist, Geoffrey Stevenson, with whom I often work, makes a practice of spending half an hour or so limbering up before he performs. Anyone using physical skills will do the same in order to attain the level of concentration and muscular co-ordination necessary for their work. Similarly, our spiritual faculties often need a 'work-out' before they are ready to function efficiently, and the time immediately prior to corporate worship is the crucial time.

Most of us lead busy lives, and a large proportion of us are far too busy, but nevertheless we are all able, if we put our minds to it, to limber up spiritually and mentally even if it is just as we walk, cycle or drive to the meeting. It is undoubtedly better to put aside five or ten minutes at home privately for this, but 'mobile' preparation is still preferable to none at all. Here are some suggestions for a spiritual 'work-out':

1. Clear the day's debris; fears, worries, sins, irritations all need to be brought to the cross and abandoned there. We should pray that the Lord will help us with those problems that still cling to us, possibly through the fellowship we are about to enjoy. Relax for a few minutes in thankfulness for the forgiveness and acceptance there is in Christ.

2. Focus upon the Lord; even use your imagination to picture him before you, welcoming you deeper into his presence. Ask him whether there are any hindrances to your entering in fully, and then ask him what would give him joy and pleasure in the worship.

3. Stir your spirit into greater action: sing, give thanks, praise, use the gift of tongues to sing or pray. (This I find to be particularly helpful when my mind is everywhere but where I want it to be!) Songs, scriptures and inspired thoughts that could have a relevance later on in the meeting may stir in your mind at this time, so take note of them.

4. Pray for one or two other people who are coming, and offer yourself to the Lord to be his servant to meet the needs of others. Pray for those who will lead the meeting. Expect at this time to be led to pray for a specific thing as the Lord inspires you.

5. Meditate briefly on a verse of Scripture; the psalms are particularly helpful in preparing us for worship.

6. Go expecting God to make himself known, reminding yourself of his promises and his desire to pour out his love upon his people.

It helps to arrive a few minutes early and as you sit, or greet people, continue what you have begun, watching, listening and trying to sense where you can give to God and those around you. As people come in, you may spot a worried face, or remember that you forgot to thank somebody, or encourage someone for something that has recently happened. It helps the atmosphere of a meeting tremendously if, as we arrive, we take the trouble to make physical, verbal, or at least eye contact with our fellow-worshippers, and in this way remind ourselves that we are coming together to worship as one body. Being a self-contained person, with a tendency to withdraw into my own world, I sometimes find this an effort, but it is one of the best ways to open the doors of our little glass capsules and prepare to breathe the same fresh spiritual 'air'.

As the meeting gets under way, there are certain good disciplines that all of us can practise quite easily, to the greater praise of God and the building up of one another. (For the purpose of these suggestions I have assumed a situation that is suitable for and open to contributions from the 'floor', though many points can be carried over to a more formal setting.)

1. Give yourself wholeheartedly to praise and worship. Determine 'I will bless the Lord'. If your heart is heavy, come honestly as you are, yet giving thanks for God's faithfulness and unchanging love, and being open to joy! We must learn to offer up our tears and pain as well as our joys; it is more costly but such sacrifices of praise are of tremendous value in the sight of God.

2. Keep listening to the Lord—when distractions come

internally or externally, offer them up to God in your own heart.

3. Listen to and make room for others. Sometimes we are so caught up in what we ourselves are thinking, feeling, wanting to sing, prophesy and so on, that we blot out what other people are saying.

4. 'Desire earnestly spiritual gifts' (1 Cor 14:1)—the general rule is that if we are apathetic about gifts of the Spirit (which could also mean that we are apathetic to the needs of those around us) we probably won't receive any to give.

5. Weigh what you hear (see 1 Cor 14:29; 1 Thess 5:21). The Lord does not ask us to absorb blindly everything said and done in corporate worship; that only opens the door to error and encourages confusion. We should hold up before the Lord what we hear, and measure it against the peace in our hearts, our knowledge of Scripture, and that sense of the Lord's voice inside us. The Lord will often give leaders a special discernment in these areas.

6. Share those thoughts, words, pictures, feelings, songs, etc. that you sense are: (a) brought alive in your consciousness by the Holy Spirit, and (b) meant to be shared at the time (be wise as some things may best be shared privately later). Beware of your own mental ruts, that is, songs, thoughts, verses etc. that you suspect are just 'stuck' in your brain. This often happens with songs, which may spring to mind for no better reason than that you have come to associate them with certain surroundings. However, don't be scared to make mistakes; it is better to contribute and be wrong than to clam up out of fear. We should create an atmosphere of trust and acceptance where no one is afraid.

7. Take action. Sometimes even when it is clear that the Lord is highlighting something, for example, a particular need for prayer, it is remarkable how we quickly move on

to the next item on the agenda, when the obvious thing to do would be to stop and take action immediately! In a media-intensive society, we must be especially careful not to treat the voice of God speaking through our corporate worship as we do background music in a supermarket—impinging marginally upon our consciousness, but not to be taken seriously or acted upon. We should treat it more like listening for announcements on a railway platform; we must be ready to take action upon what we hear because we are on an important journey and cannot afford to miss the information necessary if we are to catch the right train. We should be wary of the danger of becoming unnaturally intense in all this, and remember that the presence of God is a place of rest and joy, often fun and laughter.

It's worth the hard work and pain!

All I have said about personal discipline in worship is very simple, and accessible to all whose wills are set in the direction of pleasing God and building up the body of Christ. Yet habits of laziness, selfishness, criticism and so on are so deeply ingrained in us that learning to come to give may be harder than we expected. Nevertheless the potential of a roomful of worshippers with this giving attitude is well worth the difficulty and pain of the journey there, and best of all it has the potential of moving the very heart of God to joy and pleasure and of building up his church.

16

Can You Get There From Here?

Maurice Smith relates the true story of an occasion when he and his wife were travelling by car to a wedding without having first obtained adequate directions. Sure enough, they got lost in the London one-way systems and dead-end streets, and eventually stopped to ask three elderly gentlemen seated outside a public house for assistance. After the three had debated heatedly for some minutes—the tension in the car rising steadily as each precious second ticked by—their spokesman finally announced with some authority, 'Sorry, mate, you can't get there from here!'

That situation is not dissimilar to the experience of many Christians who, having caught a vision of where they want to go in worship and having set off enthusiastically fully expecting to get there quickly, suddenly find themselves lost in an unexpected maze of problems. Sometimes the only logical conclusion seems to be that wherever you may wish to end up, you just can't get there from where you are! With your vision fresh and vibrant in your mind of what a worshipping church should be, you step through the doors of St Bede in the Marshes and your vision bursts like a bubble, as reality stares you defiantly in the face and says 'No chance, you'll never get there from here.'

But there is of course nowhere else to start from than 'here', where we are now; and whether as individuals or a congregation, we have to come to terms with where God has put us, and believe that he can show us the route to new spiritual adventures.

This chapter is an attempt to be practical, to start from where we are and begin to move in the right direction, with some simple guiding principles. There is of course no formula or method, no pattern developed in such and such a church that we should all adopt with a guarantee of success —and for that we should thank God! There is not even a clear pattern or form for worship in the New Testament that we can follow, no A–Z on 'how to become a worshipping church'. God will continue to do a unique work in each body of believers, as led by the Holy Spirit we apply the Scriptures to our own situation. It is a walk of faith into uncharted territory, not a guided tour around a museum.

To be a worshipper

First of all let us look at what any individual can do to become a worshipper. (These points are written against the broader background of previous chapters, particularly Chapter 15.)

1. Decide to worship

Because true worship is a voluntary offering of oneself, nobody else can do it for us or make us do it. Others may teach and encourage us, but in the end we either choose freely to give it or we choose not to. Whatever the state of those around us, each one of us is responsible to God for our own gift of worship to him, and we cannot excuse ourselves or give up because others are not doing it.

2. Check the source

We have already seen that the source of worship is the Holy Spirit himself, like a bubbling spring of water inside us. If you have never experienced the release of the Spirit within, then you will not know what it is to tap that divine flow, and you will soon run dry. The gift of the Holy Spirit in all his power and fullness is the birthright of every believer in Christ, so come and ask! Jesus said in Luke 11:13 (NASB), 'If you then being evil, know how to give good gifts to your children, how much more shall your heavenly Father give the Holy Spirit to those who ask him?' If you experience difficulty in receiving as I did, then go for advice and prayer. Many of us who for many years have been 'born again' have never claimed this part of our birthright, and look on baffled and uncertain at those who are obviously overflowing from the inside.

3. Go on being filled

When we are commanded in Ephesians 5:18 to 'be filled with the Spirit', the tense is the present continuous—in other words, it means 'be being filled', or 'continually be filled' with the Spirit. It is not enough to look back to an initial experience and, as it were, dip our cup into the bucket we filled some time ago. Spring water is the water of this moment, fresh and sparkling. Yesterday's water is brackish and soon runs out. We must learn to encourage a steady flow of the Spirit by obedience, love and good deeds, thanksgiving and praise.

4. Practise in private

Even if we find ourselves in churches where overt expressions of praise are frowned upon, we can make up for our public restrictions by letting rip in private! Whether we shut ourselves away in a bedroom, head for solitude in the countryside, or drive alone in the car, most of us if we try can make time alone in which we can sing, dance, pray aloud and generally express our worship without psychological damage to others! Also, it is often easier to break down personal inhibitions and to experiment with richer forms of expression in private first.

5. Worship with others

Better still, there may be opportunities in small prayer cells, house groups and so on where a number of people may share the same concern for worship and feel safe enough with one another to break new ground. Individual worship is important, but, like the footballer who practises in the backyard knows, the real thrills come when you're playing with the team.

6. Replace old habits

If on each occasion when we normally grumbled, complained or entertained negative thoughts, we decided instead to give thanks and praise, we would be well on the way to offering up our everyday lives in worship to God. Old habits usually only die when we replace them with new ones, and while the power to change comes from God, the choice to change is ours. That decision may come a hundred times a day, when we make the choice between following our old patterns or substituting new ones.

Can we get there from here—together?

If we are to make progress in our worship, there is no escaping the prospect of change. With change comes conflict, and we are often afraid of both. If, however, we want to avoid change and conflict, then we must of necessity avoid Christ as well, because his kingdom only grows as his people radically change to become like him, and the stronger it gets the more it conflicts with rival kingdoms, whether of men or of Satan. Worship of the kind I have attempted to describe in this book, which consumes our whole being, is at the same time a gentle and a dangerous thing.

True worship is bound to reveal more of the character of Jesus, and he is described in Scripture as both a Lion and a Lamb. If our worship is to become real, then this is who will walk among us, at times in gentleness and at times in fearsome grandeur. I long, and at the same time rightly fear, to hear more of the mighty roar of the Lion of Judah in our worship, for there is a need in our times to regain first-hand knowledge of the awesome majesty and power of Jesus. Judah in fact means 'praise', so Jesus is literally the Lion of praise, as well as the sacrificial lamb who was led meekly to the slaughter. Ultimately, the central issue in our decision to pursue true worship is whether or not we are willing for this Jesus to walk among us as our King. If we are indeed willing, then we have begun the journey.

Some guiding principles

Tens of thousands of Christians find themselves either becalmed in an atmosphere of apathy, or caught up in a cross-current of differing traditions, beliefs and opinions about worship; there is no doubt that when the prospect of change comes, people are divided over how it should be done and what form it should take. There are, however, certain principles that, when applied, may make the difference between getting there together or fragmenting in the process.

Worship is a response

As I have said elsewhere, it is impossible to draw rich worship from poverty-stricken hearts, and we must be careful not to change the externals before people's own experience of God is renewed. Worship should develop alongside spiritual growth, both expressing it and stimulating it, but if we merely impose new styles and methods on top of a dead situation, we will end up with nothing better than the equivalent of a beautifully decorated coffin! Changes of a deep and real kind do not come overnight; as I have often heard it said, God does not plant bombs, he plants trees!

I was speaking quite recently to a woman who prayed for eight years over the vision of her church becoming a renewed worshipping community before she could conclude that her prayers had been answered. The noisy background to our conversation was a tremendous service of joyful worship in her church, which would have been unthinkable eight years before! I am sure many have prayed for much longer and are still praying, but how many of us have given up after two years, or one year, or six months!

Another church I know endured an organist who resisted all forms of change and heartfelt worship for seven years before he finally resigned. During this time they were experiencing renewal, but decided to be loving and patient with him hoping that he would eventually become part of what God was doing. One day he stormed out and never came back, but meanwhile the Spirit had been doing a deep work in the hearts of the congregations such that when the freedom came, there was a maturity in them to make wise use of their new liberty.

The fruit of the Spirit is ... patience

There is of course a limit to how long we should wait for a group of believers to be willing and able to worship 'in spirit and in truth', because it would appear that in some places the waiting will go on for ever! The question of how long we should wait is not one to which any of us can give a standard answer, and indeed if God worked to a published timetable in these matters, I suspect that most of us would still miss the train! We must remember that each church, though part of a much greater plan, is a unique creation in the hands of the Builder, and it is our closeness to him and our listening to his plans that will enable us to build according to his time-scale. There is no doubt that with motivation and ingenuity, even impatience and aggression, we can build something. However, though wood, hay and stubble (1 Cor 3:12) are always near to hand and easy to scratch together into something resembling a dwelling place, gold is a totally different proposition. Gold is a hidden treasure that can only be mined with commitment and patience, and it is with spiritual 'gold' that Jesus builds his church. Patience, however, should not be confused with complacency. Rather, it is a quality that overflows from the Spirit within us. It is logical then that if we are drawing upon the Lord's patience in our situation, we will naturally be in tune with what he is doing.

Be honest, what is your motive?

The right motives and attitudes are vital if change is not to cause unnecessary friction and pain, and we need to be honest with ourselves and alert to the deceit of our own hearts. In your dreams and imaginations of glorious worship in your church, do you feature as the hero, or at least the one who gets a fair slice of the credit? Do you gloat over visions of your opponents or rivals shamed and humbled before you? Or of the retreat to other fellowships of 'stick-in-the-muds' and 'traditionalists'? Do you mentally draw up plans and budgets for recording and distributing your tape of 'home-grown' worship songs that will at least put your fellowship on the ecclesiastical map? None of us is immune to these mixed motives, and such things have often featured in my daydreams! Thankfully the Lord does not wait until our motives are 100% pure or else he would have to wait for ever, but he takes us as we are, gently but firmly turning up the heat of the Refiner's fire, bringing yet more impurities to the surface to be skimmed off.

It is vital, however, that our dominant motive should be the desire to see God worshipped, because to have any other dominant motive is idolatry and therefore a contradiction of what true worship is. If we are to be agents of change, we must be sure that we are first of all instruments in his hands, not mavericks kicking up a lot of dust and dirt to nobody's advantage.

A contrite, humble spirit

Those whom God chooses to bring about change, he draws closer to himself and plants his concerns in their heart and his love in their behaviour. A place of worship is a place close to God's heart and we read in Isaiah 57:15 in the Living Bible of the kind of people who are 'at home' there: 'The high and lofty one who inhabits eternity, the Holy One, says this "I live in the high and holy place where those with contrite, humble spirits dwell."' A concern for worship in that holy place cannot be severed from the contrite humble spirit of the servant. Our attitude must be submissive, gentle and sympathetic, sensitive and loving, yet courageous and with a godly determination. We must put aside bitterness and rivalry, genuinely seeking God's glory, not fighting for position and influence. The alternative may be to discover that though our aims were commendable and our doctrine biblical, our attitude has caused us to end up wrestling with God when we thought we were wrestling with his enemies.

Don't let your concern for, or role in, worship become your 'extended ego'. While we are genuinely serving God's interests we are not nearly so likely to become personally offended, jealous or insecure. If a position of responsibility is given to you, hold it lightly as something that is on trust from God and not your own possession. A servant is also one whose ear is alert for others, so listen to God and one another.

But I couldn't possibly...

The opposite of the 'extended ego' is the 'inverted ego', and it is probable that more of us suffer from that than the former. Most churches contain people who hide their talents, often out of lack of confidence. Feeling that they have little to offer, they do not even offer the little they have, and often the 'little' is in reality a great deal! One of the most valuable ministries in the church must surely be the ability to draw out hidden gifts and to encourage people who do not realize they have anything to offer.

To pray is to change things

In our impatience, we find it easier to rush ahead and act upon our plans and impulses than to pray. We often make the mistake of regarding prayer as a way of suspending action, a hindrance to 'getting down to the nitty gritty'. In fact, real prayer does suspend a certain kind of action, and that is action that arises out of impatience, frustration, selfish ambition, good intentions and the like. In prayer we have to stop and listen, check our motives, and sense the Spirit praying his concerns through ourselves and other people. It also causes us to look for indications of divine activity, and as we see our prayers answered we can more easily identify the nature of the unique work of grace that God is doing among us.

To pray is to 'tune into' what God is doing, and then we can proceed with divinely initiated plans. It is to enter into that rest which comes when we work according to the power of God working in us, and the strategy which he knows will succeed. In matters of conflict with other people, prayer opens us up to perceive God's perspective of them, and we will become more able to share his love, understanding and patience. We will also be faced with our own prejudices and faults and learn to understand the difficulties other people have with us!

Get to know one another

To worship in truth is to open ourselves up, to be real and honest before God and one another, and express what is inside us. This kind of worship involves a lowering of barriers, and making ourselves vulnerable. This is difficult to do among strangers when there may be fear of misunderstanding, betrayal of trust and so on. Hence it is an essential background to the growth of worship in a fellowship that we are getting to know one another as ordinary people, and developing an atmosphere of 'belonging'. It also counteracts any tendency we may have to use the forms of worship as an escape from being real with one another. Meetings are not always suitable places for getting to know people personally, so build friendships in each other's homes, through pursuing common interests and caring practically for one another's needs.

Walk together

In any group of Christians there will be those who are impatient to steam on ahead in worship, those who move at a steady pace, and those who trail or limp slowly behind. It is a mark of our love for one another that we should adjust our pace so that we can walk together. Those who wish to rush ahead must sometimes stop to encourage the stragglers, the healthy must allow the lame to lean on them, and the lazy must stir themselves to move faster. If we are to grow in worship as a united body, we have to sacrifice our independence and make the journey together.

Worship blossoms in an atmosphere of love

If you want worship to develop, do your part in causing love to grow, because worship is like the beautiful blossom on a fruitful tree and the roots of our 'tree' must be in a deep love for one another.

Encourage a 'family' atmosphere

Not only is it conducive to worship to promote a sense of the church being a large family, it is also conducive to worship to encourage family worship of a literal kind. People are much more relaxed and open and prepared to accept change and innovation when children are involved in services. It is also worth pondering that if our celebration of knowing Christ is way over the heads of children, then it is possible that we ourselves are not coming like little children, but as cool, detached, sophisticated adults.

Get under cover!

While ideas about, and practices of, leadership and authority vary enormously, the Scriptures make it clear that we should all be in an attitude of submission. In Ephesians 5:21 we read, 'Submit to one another out of reverence for Christ.' It is out of reverence for Christ because Christ lives within each one of us, both individually and corporately, and though opinions, characters and personalities differ, we must listen for his voice in one another. Christ himself was under authority, and his conversation with the Roman centurion in Matthew 8:9 indicates that true spiritual authority is only given to those who are themselves under it. God will not trust us with the authority to bring about changes and to build his kingdom if we are loners and one-man-bands, doing our own thing.

There is great safety in being under an 'umbrella' of love from other Christians whose concern it is to help, guide and protect us, and if those people are also the ones with gifts and callings of leadership, then the possibility of moving a whole fellowship further in worship is wide open. Towards leaders and among leaders there should be respect, trust, communication, friendship, humility and flexibility, and all these can be summed up in the word 'love'.

Serve the people

It is important for those who lead in worship to act as servants of the people. It is impossible in such a position to avoid putting a personal 'stamp' of style, taste and so on upon the worship, but we must be careful not to impose it. The worship should be a genuine expression of the people, and a good look at them will illustrate their variety, which in turn implies variety of taste, style and culture. To serve the people involves enabling as many of them as possible to express themselves in ways that they can relate to or can readily learn to relate to. We must serve the old as well as the young, the conservative as well as the adventurous, those brought up in the old traditions as well as those brought in on contemporary worship choruses. If a heart for worship is present among the people, then God can be worshipped equally well in a variety of cultural and stylistic settings, as long as the material chosen successfully expresses spiritual life and truth relevant to the church at the time. The choice of style, musical setting and similar considerations are as much pastoral matters as musical ones, and have a strong influence in either uniting or polarizing people in worship.

Make God central

This may seem like an obvious thing to do, because making God central is what worship is all about, but it is very easy in a climate of change for the issues surrounding the practice of worship to dominate our thoughts instead of God himself. While we need to give attention to the principles and mechanics of worship, it is only a revelation of God that causes it to flow out of thankful and wondering hearts. There is an important principle embodied in Jesus' words recorded in John 12:32—'But I, when I am lifted up from the earth, will draw all men to myself.' A divine magnetism comes into operation when we see the kind of God that we have, One who took on human flesh and was crucified for our sake.

If through the preaching that we hear, the Scriptures that we read, and the testimonies that we share, the grace of God in Christ Jesus is revealed to us, then worship will be ignited in us. If we are asking people to worship, we must give them cause to, by lifting up before them a God

whose character and deeds deserve no less than the best
worship we can offer.

264
K33L

88549

LINCOLN CHRISTIAN COLLEGE AND SEMINARY

264
K33L   Kendrick, Graham.
            Learning to
         worship as a way of
         life
                        88549

DEMCO